LAURA
AS NOVEL, FILM, AND MYTH

Over-the-mantel portrait of Laura. The artist was in love with her when he painted it and Detective McPherson fell in love with the image.

"LAURA" © Twentieth Century Fox Film Corporation. All rights reserved. 1944

LAURA
AS NOVEL, FILM, AND MYTH

Eugene McNamara

The Edwin Mellen Press
Lewiston/Queenston/Lampeter

Library of Congress Cataloging-in-Publication Data

McNamara, Eugene.
   'Laura' as novel, film, and myth / Eugene McNamara.
     p.   cm.
   Includes bibliographical references.

   1. Laura (Motion picture) 2. Caspary, Vera,. 1904-1987. Laura.
3. Caspary, Vera, 1904-1987--Film and video adaptations. I. Title.
PN1997.L3473M38 1992
791.43'72--dc20   92-6560
ISBN 0-7734-0838-X   CIP

A CIP catalog record for this book
is available from the British Library.

Copyright © 1992 Eugene McNamara

All rights reserved. For information contact

The Edwin Mellen Press   The Edwin Mellen Press
      Box 450   Box 67
Lewiston, New York   Queenston, Ontario
    USA 14092   CANADA L0S 1L0

The Edwin Mellen Press, Ltd.
Lampeter, Dyfed, Wales
UNITED KINGDOM SA48 7DY

Printed in the United States of America

When from the long distant past nothing subsists, after the people are dead, after the things are broken and scattered, still alone, more fragile, but with more vitality, more unsubstantial, yet more persistent, more faithful, the smell and taste of things remain poised for a long time, like souls, ready to remind us, waiting and hoping for their moment, amid the ruins of all the rest and bear unfalteringly, in the most impalpable drop of their essence, the vast structure of recollection.

--Proust

This book is for Margaret.

CONTENTS

Page

Acknowledgements	i
Introduction	ii
One: The Film	1
Two: The Novel	21
Three: Production	37
Four: Final Take and Launch, and Other Venues and Spinoffs	55
Still Photos	69
Conclusion	73
Bibliography	89
Index	93

ACKNOWLEDGMENTS

LAURA
Johnny Mercer & David Raksin
Copyright (c) 1945 (Renewed 1973) TWENTIETH CENTURY MUSIC CORPORATION   All Rights Controlled by ROBBINS MUSIC CORPORATION   All Rights of ROBBINS MUSIC CORPORATION Assigned to EMI CATALOGUE PARTNERSHIP   All Rights Administered by EMI ROBBINS CATALOG INC.
International Copyright Secured Made in U.S.A.
All Rights Reserved

I am grateful to Dr. Stuart Selby, Professor, Department of Communication Studies at the University of Windsor and Dr. Donald McCaffery, Professor of English at the University of North Dakota for reading and reviewing my book before it went to press.

I wish to express my gratitude to the following individuals and institutions who were generous in helping me explore the *Laura* mystique: David Raksin, Joseph La Shelle, Dana Andrews, ASCAP, The Margaret Herrick Library of The Academy of Motion Picture Arts and Sciences, UCLA Library, The Dallas Public Library, the Theatre and Film Section of the Metropolitan Toronto Library and The University of Windsor. Thanks to Colleen Cassano who helped me with the hardware, which was hard. I thank my daughter, Mary McNamara, who suggested that I write the book and traced some difficult to find material. And I thank my wife, Margaret, who was always more sure than I was that it would be written.

INTRODUCTION

*We may not remember what Laura was like,
but we never forget that she* was *the music.*
--Elmer Bernstein

This book is a study of the 1944 film *Laura,* the 1943 novel on which it was based, the various scripts that came between the novel and film, the story of the production, the film's reception and its subsequent history. In Johnny Mercer's lyrics for the music David Raksin wrote for the movie, Laura is a "face in the misty light", a haunting, elusive, dream-like figure.

Laura as seen in the novel, the scripts and the film exhibits a number of different character traits. Put together, they do not add up and none of them taken by itself is a satisfying, complete explanation of who Laura *is.* Laura is a protean figure, tantalizing, evanescent. She is, in fact, a mythic figure. And the film is mythopoeic.

There have not been at the time of this writing any remakes. There were several television versions, based on the stage play which was mounted after the film was released. Neither the stage play nor the television attempts were as successful or as satisfying as the film--or, indeed, the novel. There are elements in this film which make it unique. The merging of story, setting, character, direction and cinematography created a classic work of art which stands alone, *sui generis.* A remake, or colorization, would be irrelevant.

The film has been called "a cool piece of work, silken, remote, perhaps the most posh of all *films noirs.*"[1] And it has been called a "cult classic and revival house favorite."[2] It has inspired other films:

---

[1] Foster Hirsch, *The Dark Side of the Screen: Film Noir* (San Diego, New York: A.S. Barnes, 1981), p. 121.

[2] Danny Peary, *Cult Movies* (New York: Delacorte, 1981), p. 199.

Vertigo, Sharkey's Machine and *Someone to Watch Over Me*.

But seldom has a film which became a classic--cult, *noir* or whatever--had such an unpromising beginning. Otto Preminger had been interested in the story since the novel was published. He offered to help author Vera Caspary with the stage version. When he went to Twentieth Century Fox he persuaded the studio to buy the movie rights. Studio boss Darryl F. Zanuck was lukewarm about the project, told Preminger that he could produce it, but would not be allowed to direct it. Zanuck assigned the picture a "B" budget. He kept interfering, waffling, making suggestions on casting, asking for script changes. Eventually he elevated the project to "A" status and gave Preminger the ok to direct. Down to the wire, he was asking for changes and felt, on the film's wrap, that he might have a dud on his hands.

At Oscar time, all Zanuck's publicity efforts went to his big, "serious", "important" movie *Wilson*. Two and a half hours long. Five point two million dollars to make it. *Wilson* received critical respect and a respectable boxoffice. It got ten Academy Award nominations. *Laura* received five. Both films lost to *Going My Way* which swept all the contenders off the set. *Laura* won for Best Black and White cinematography. Its only Oscar. It wasn't nominated for Best Picture. Raksin's score was not nominated either.

I do not think anybody today would call *Wilson* or *Going My Way* a classic, cult or otherwise. But *Laura* continues to have its audience. The film's score, set with lyrics by Johnny Mercer, has had its own separate career. It is the second-most recorded popular song of all time.

What is the essence of *Laura's* unique mystique? There are a number of discernable factors. First is the character of the woman herself. She is, as said above, elusive and tantalizing. She is every romantic adolescent's dream woman. One need not be adolescent in age to feel the pull of this attraction. It is not "sex goddess", "sex kitten" or any other kind of purely physical appeal. It belongs somewhere in the neighborhood of yet-unformed prepubescent longings and what Dante saw in Beatrice.

Secondly there is the story itself as seen on the screen. Posh settings, witty dialogue and a mystery to be solved. The story is half police procedure and half duel of verbal wit. Like other Forties mysteries its plot convolutions parallel a tortured thought process. *Why* becomes more important than *who*. Unlike the gangster dramas of the Thirties, where clear lines were drawn between good and evil, between those inside and outside the law, the Forties crime stories blurred the lines. A Thirties detective would never fall in love with a dead woman's image. Nor would there be any doubt about who was a good girl and who wasn't. The bad girl was always followed by saxophone music.

When we learn that the victim--the girl murdered by mistake in Laura's place--was a model named Diane Redfern, we are not roused to speculation about *her* character. Laura has been set off by herself as a special problem.

Vera Caspary created a complicated, mercurial modern woman. In the film she loses some of the complication. First she is seen as a love-struck painter saw her when he did her portrait. She is wistful, dewy eyed, one hand delicately just below her throat, the other hand hanging down languidly. She is imagined by the detective as a two-timing "dame" who was probably murdered by a lover she deceived. Then the detective falls under the absent woman's charm and he falls in love with the painter's image. Finally Laura returns to life but her behavior is erratic and arouses suspicion. Is Laura capable of murder as well as being capable of deception?

In Vera Caspary's novel *Laura* there are two objects which become symbols which help express the story's theme. The first is Waldo Lydecker's antique walking stick. He always carries it. It is part of his persona. But hidden in the stick is a shotgun, the murder weapon. Caspary said that she meant the stick to be a rather obviously Freudian symbol for Lydecker's impotence.

The second object is a mercury coated glass globe, part of Lydecker's glass collection. It is a reflecting and distorting device, and it also, like the walking stick, hides something. The glass is weighted with buckshot, the ammunition used in the murder. Waldo's second attempt to kill Laura ends in shattering the globe. The glass globe does not appear in the film. The murder weapon is a mundane shotgun hidden in an antique French clock. In place of the motifs of impotence, hidden danger and duplicity, the film uses repeated images to express theme.

One of these repeated images is detective Mark McPherson *almost* smiling on five different occasions. Habitually the detective's face is set in stoic cop grimness. So when he almost smiles, but swiftly smothers it, he gives us a brief glimpse of a vulnerable human being hidden inside the facade of justice.

The first time is in the opening scene, where we see him standing in the midst of Lydecker's exquisite apartment, obviously not overwhelmed, hat kept on at a tough angle, cigarette dangling. He almost smiles, or smirks. Later in this scene he interrogates Lydecker who is typing in his bathtub. Lydecker asks him to hand him a towel. McPherson hands the towel off camera and almost smiles again. Both times he had almost smiled in judgement: he shows contempt for too much wealth and taste and contempt for someone naked, old and thin. The first reaction is that of the proletarian, the second is less admirable. It echoes crude macho posing. But both times McPherson almost smiling has served to reinforce opposition in two types of character. One is the tough, physical man of action and the other the aesthete whose chief weapon is verbal wit.

The next time McPherson almost smiles is just after Laura returns and wakes him up. After she goes to her room to change a look of joy suffuses his face and he almost smiles. Just before he leaves her that night he asks whether or not she is going to marry Shelby Carpenter. When she says no, he almost smiles but just as swiftly suppresses it.

After a party to celebrate Laura's rebirth, McPherson takes her to headquarters where he submits her to harsh questioning. She admits that she pretended to continue her engagement to Shelby only to protect him. No, she says, she does not love Shelby. McPherson has to smother another almost-smile.

In these two scenes with Laura, McPherson reveals himself as a man struggling with himself. One part of him is the official face of the law. "I suspect everyone," he says, "And no one." But behind the stern official face is the man who could fall in love with an image, who is in love with the living woman. In these three scenes, then, McPherson expresses subtle nuances of character: no nonsense proletarian, locker room braggart, vulnerable romantic.

Waldo Lydecker also has two recurring scenes, which, like McPherson's smiles, help express his character. Both are in the bathtub, naked, sitting in tepid water, typing. Our first glimpse of Waldo is in the opening scene. The bathroom is lavishly Art Deco, the bathtub sunken. Waldo is not sitting in the tub for hygienic reasons. A typewriter on a swivel table swings in front of him. Seated like a Roman Emperor, he can cool off and type hot copy.

The second bathtub scene is after he discovers Jacoby, the man who painted Laura's portrait, leaving her apartment. It is a cold, snowy winter night. But Waldo hurries home to stay up all night writing a column. Middle of winter. Obviously it isn't just to beat the heat.

Lolling in the tub may express hedonism, or it may be a sign of infantilism. The sight of Lydecker naked in his bathroom brought a wry smirk to McPherson's lips. He was equally contemptuous of the interior decoration in the living room. A deleted voiceover has McPherson comment that the taste exhibited was "too exquisite for a man."

Some of Lydecker's mannerisms and his platonic detached relationship with Laura may hint at homosexuality. In fact studio boss Zanuck was afraid that Clifton Webb was too overtly effeminate for the role. McPherson's disdain for Lydecker's too fussy taste and love of watery comfort can be seen as Forties views of what a "real" man's attitudes towards *anything* which might be taken as homosexual should be.

But all this is misleading. What to make of Waldo's jealous possessiveness? What to make of his attempt to kill her? What is his motive, if he is, in fact, homosexual? The bathtub scenes may give evidence of narcissism or infantilism or mere eccentricity. Neither his fondness for the tub nor his collection of antiques, or his dandy-style dressing and caustic wit are evidence of perversion.

Such attributes *were* sometimes used as code signals in Production Code days. Take Joel Cairo's perfumed handkerchief in *The Maltese Falcon* for example.

But in *Laura* they were used in a new way to express sophistication. And perhaps they were used to mask Lydecker's hidden motive: a man's murderous fury caused by his inability to possess what he cannot.

Some women do seek the company of homosexual men. They find the men unthreatening, safe, amusing. In most male-female relationships friendship is a precarious state. Either it escalates towards something more serious or it burns out. Friendships between women and homosexual men however, can be longer-lived, free of the anxiety of sexual possibilities.

But Laura is not the kind of woman to seek the safety of a homosexual's friendship. She does not use Lydecker as a means of escaping heterosexual romances. Lydecker does all he can to destroy her romances. Her feelings for Lydecker are a genuine mix of fondness, admiration and gratitude.

Part of McPherson's problem, aside from finding the murderer, is finding out who Laura is. His problem becomes the film viewer's too. Laura's character is *not* developed by recurring scenes. McPherson's hat, set at a tough angle, and his baseball puzzle game accentuate the times his stoic countenance is almost broken by a smile. The hat and game are parallel props to Lydecker's homburg, carnation in the buttonhole and walking stick.

The fedora is proletarian cop, the homburg uptown. The fresh carnation is conspicuous consumption as well as aestheticism. So is the walking stick. Along with Lydecker's penchant for typing in the tub, all his visual code clues support his dialogue. The two characters, complete with value systems, are clearly set in opposition.

Laura is given no visual code signals to wear. Shelby at one point admires her hat (McPherson *never* would have) but he also, in another scene, admires Anne Treadwell's hat, which is dreadful. The admiration is "noticing," an attribute of sitting in critical judgment. Or it may be a flirt's ploy.

Laura's hat and the rest of her clothing is conventionally correct. However, although a career woman, she does not wear big shouldered tailored suits. Little in her apartment or in her cottage seems to individualize her. She is the result of a number of points of view.

Part of *Laura*'s continuing pull is nostalgia. The film seems set in a more innocent time. Pre television, pre AIDS, pre Vietnam, pre assassinations. Oh there was crime and evil. This was, after all, a murder story. But one could walk the streets of New York at any hour in safety. At least one did in movies. It was a time when only jazz musicians used drugs, or were reputed to do so. Cops could freely use the third degree. Killers got the hot seat. Men wore hats. Maids were not uppity.

But *Laura* was a World War Two era film. The time of the story is indefinite but appears to be contemporary. Yet no mention is made of the war. In the following year, in *The Big Sleep* detective Philip Marlowe has a "B" gas ration sticker on his car window. When Marlowe calls his pal Bernie Ohls at headquarters to report another corpse he jokes about having some more "red stamps." This refers to meat rationing tokens. Audiences today might miss those little allusions.

But there are none to miss in *Laura*. The story seems free-floating, connected to nothing specifically temporary.

Critics have remarked on Otto Preminger's elegant directing and fluid camera work. As John Belton put it:

> The unobtrusive, orderly but effortless elegance of his compositions reflects a complex sensibility in tune with both the refined, restrained passions of his characters and with a larger sphere of emotional experiences that goes beyond articulation. Each character in a Preminger film serves as a fragment of an overall design; much like separate, straight lines that run endlessly through space without touching one another, his characters exist independently of each other, self-contained and self sufficient.[3]

Certainly the characters in *Laura* bear out Belton's thesis. Laura and McPherson exchange one chaste kiss. McPherson punches Shelby in the belly. A policeman shoots Lydecker. That is about it as far as vigorous action goes. Mostly the characters enter or leave a room or stand, grouped, in the room. Even together they exude a strong sense of isolation.

Time and space in *Laura* is very tight. The running time is eighty-eight minutes. The action is over a weekend and a few days. And the treatment of space in the film is an important factor contributing to its final effect. Most of *Laura*'s action is indoors. There are very few exterior scenes and when they exist, they are brief bridging structures to another interior.

There are no open roads, vast skies, mountain ranges or fields of grain in *Laura*. There was a baseball stadium sequence in the final script. McPherson was annoyed because the Laura Hunt case interferred with his day off and his plans to go to a ball game. He bullies Lydecker and Carpenter into going with him, continuing his

---

[3]John Belton, *Cinema Stylists* (Metuchen, N.J., 1983), p. 205.

interrogation as the game goes on. Still pictures exist of this sequence, indicating that it may have been shot, but it was deleted from the final film. McPherson finds a baseball on Laura's desk, is puzzled by it, puts it down and no more is made of it. What remains of baseball in the screened film is a puzzle game that McPherson plays with to keep his nerves calm.

"Use lots of mirrors," Alfred Hitchcock said to set decorator Henry Bumstead before they began work on *Vertigo*. *Laura*'s settings are full of mirrors. Like portraits, mirrors are double images. They suggest an inherent confusion between the real thing and the image. Mirrors also suggest narcissism. Remember Snow White's stepmother.

The crowded, claustral interior spaces in *Laura* contribute to a heightened psychological state of frustration and entrapment. Like Laura herself, the audience feels hemmed inside an airless world of fussy, crowded interior decoration.

Many of the brief exterior scenes are at night. During the daytime, sunlight comes in only through drawn venetian blinds. The ensuing mood is one of unnatural, artificial, deceptive, inauthentic paranoia.

Description of chapters:

Chapter One. The Film. This chapter is a close reading, an exegesis of the film as seen on screen. The movie opens with a framed portrait of a woman and the title *Laura* superimposed on it. The "Laura" theme music swells up. This initial visual-aural-print metaphor, immediately established, is elaborated on throughout the film. In this first chapter, each scene is examined for its metaphoric, visual and thematic content. The film is also placed in its genre and some speculation is made about why it continues to exert a unique and powerful effect on viewers.

Chapter Two. The Novel. This chapter is an equally close study of Vera Caspary's 1943 novel, *Laura*, on which the film was based. Immediately apparent differences between the film's plot and characterization and the novel's are noted and reasons for the differences are advanced.

The novel's characters are different from the film's. Waldo Lydecker is obese and impotent in the novel, wasp-waisted and enigmatic in the film. The detective, Mark McPherson, is a complex figure in the novel, but little more than a simple gumshoe in the film. The biggest change is in Laura. The novel's complicated modern woman is little more than an icon, like her portrait, in the film.

Plot incidents and narrative devices are altered or eliminated in the process of moving from novel to film. Much of the novel's aesthetic effect is swallowed up in translation. Yet something remains--altered, still effective in its own way.

Chapter Three. The Production. This is a chronicle of the film's creation--from buying the rights to casting, choice of and dismissal of director, casting negotiation, compromises, in-fighting, ego expanding and deflation, the converging of chance, accident and invention. The scripts--from First Draft to Final Script--*and* further re-written scenes--are discussed and compared, with some speculation on why changes were made or not made.

Chapter Four. Describes the film's initial reception. Critics and public were warm but not ecstatic. Clifton Webb was nominated for an Oscar. He did not win. Johnny Mercer wrote the words for the film's score and the song went on to become the second-most recorded popular song of all time.

Laura has had its tributes and influence: *Sharkey's Machine* and *Someone to Watch Over Me* are examples. *Laura* has been spoofed on Carol Burnett and was the inspiration for a *Magnum P.I.* episode.

Originally planned as a stage play, *Laura* finally got written for stage and was mounted twice in the U.S. and once in England. There have been two television productions. Neither the stage nor television productions were as successful as the 1944 film. This chapter closely discusses the theatrical versions of *Laura* in terms of structure, character and theme.

The Conclusion extrapolates on the image of Laura as icon, fatal woman, dream fantasy and goddess. Obviously the story has strong psychological and mythic undertones.

LAURA
AS NOVEL, FILM, AND MYTH

ONE: THE FILM

"Use lots of mirrors."

--Alfred Hitchcock giving advice to his set designer on *Vertigo*.

The film opens with the one-word title superimposed on a large portrait of Laura hanging over a fireplace. David Raksin's haunting score is heard. An immediate connection is thus made among Laura's visual image, her name and the music. The name suggests Petrarch's Fourteenth Century Laura, who became in his sonnets a symbol of passion for idealized and unattainable beauty. Vera Caspary says that she was not influenced by the allusion or, indeed, much interested in the literary tradition that came after Petrarch which includes Byron and Schiller. She simply liked the name.[1]

The 1944 audience might well have been reminded of another film with a woman's first name as title: *Rebecca* (1938). It too begins with a voiceover narration. There is a dead woman's portrait hanging in a prominent place and her absence is a paradoxical presence haunting the living. *Rebecca* also expressed the theme of obsessive and destructive love.

The portrait of Laura is a Sargentesque study, evoking glamor and elegance as well as beauty. It never occurs to any of the characters in the film that the act of hanging one's own portrait in an important place on a wall in one's own home could be regarded as narcissistic. And, unlike Eliot's "Portrait of a Lady" and all the other sardonic portraits of the early modern period (Joyce's, Henry James's, Pound's) the portrait of Laura is not meant to be ironic. It is meant to function as a contemporary version of Poe's Helen, an icon of eternal beauty which remains forever out of reach.

---

[1] Rudy Behlmer, *America's Favorite Movies: Behind the Scenes* (New York: Ungar, 1982), p. 177.

Other films that use the painting motif include, besides *Rebecca, Vertigo, Portrait of Jennie* and *Woman in the Window*. Portraits, like mirror images, (except that the portraits are idealized and improved) express the idea of Duality. Perhaps *The Picture of Dorian Gray* (1945) is the most well-known expression of the duality motif in film history. Dorian's portrait changed with every sin he committed while he remained as perfect as a work of art.

Raksin's Laura theme will not be heard again for some time. It is not romantic music used to adumbrate and enhance a love scene. It is never played under a two-shot of Laura and McPherson. Thus it remains attached to Laura alone, adding to the cluster of visual images expressing mystery, evanescence and the enigmatic unattainable quality she evokes.

The theme is never played all the way through. This emphasizes Laura's paradoxical absence which is a pervasive presence. Unresolved music equals ephemeral woman. The unfinished music also suggests the pain of lost or unrequited love, perpetual longing: an aching tension which is never released.

A different kind of music is heard under the opening scene--brooding, foreboding menace. We see a tastefully decorated room, dimly lit by light coming in through Venetian blinds. An oriental figure stands in a niche. There is a wall with a collection of masks on it. A collection of glass objects is displayed in a glass case. Through this case we can see a tall antique clock. The total effect of the setting is of wealth and taste. But the music, low and somber, goes along with Waldo Lydecker's voiceover narration:

> I shall never forget this weekend--the weekend Laura died. A silver sun burned through the sky like a huge magnifying glass... It was the hottest Sunday in my recollection. I felt as if I were the only human being left in New York. And in a sense it was true. For with Laura's horrible death I was alone...

Some of the objects seen in this opening scene will develop symbolically. Like the oriental figure in the niche, Laura becomes (when later reborn) a poised, posed figure. Her physical motion is severely limited. Mainly, she stands in the centers of various rooms, as if pressed in on all sides by her possessions, her achieved status, and her putative friends and lovers. Like the collection of masks on Waldo's wall, the friends and lovers hide their real feelings.

Waldo's voiceover in this scene is the last remaining vestige of Caspary's three first person narrators in the novel, maintained through all the scripts but dropped from the final film. This opening sequence may be the only vestige of Rouben Mamoulian's work left in the final film. Otto Preminger reshot the rest of Mamoulian's scenes.

The opening scene suggests, through the slow sweeping inventory of beautiful objects, the brooding menacing music and Waldo's cultured, melancholy and poetic language the theme of danger lurking under an attractive veneer. Waldo's narration ends with "...another of those detectives" as we see Mark McPherson standing in the midst of all the tasteful decor, looking at the wall decorated with a collection of masks. There is a twitch of an amused smile on his face.

He is a modern gumshoe, a fedora hat set at a brash angle. A cigarette dangles from his lips, completing the physical posture of contempt for all the fussiness. The tall antique clock strikes and McPherson is galvanized into cop action: notebook out, he crosses over to the clock, checking the time against his wristwatch. Does the antique clock work as well as look pretty? McPherson's gesture with his watch sums up the collision of values--realistic pragmatism set against traditionalism and aestheticism. And the clock is established in the audience's visual imagination. We will later learn that the murder gun is hidden in a matching clock in Laura's apartment. The sequence ends with the detective sliding the glass cabinet's door open to pick up a piece of objet d' art and Waldo's warning call that the "stuff is priceless" coming from another room.

The opening scene expresses the theme of pragmatic street reality in opposition to rich elegance. Class distinctions are at times subtle and then overt in this film. McPherson, the detective, moves at will through the haute world, given entrée because a murder has been committed and he has momentary power. But it is uneasy power. It takes great force of will and stoic detachment on McPherson's part. Above all, it calls for strict adherence to his code in order to keep psychic balance.

McPherson is both amused and contemptuous of the uptown world. Bessie, Laura's maid, in contrast stands for complete surrender to it. Her devotion to Laura would work well if the movie were an antebellum romance, and Laura were a belle and Bessie herself were a shuffling darkie. Bessie is used and patronized by everybody in the movie. She knows her place. She and McPherson (and a few shadowy policemen, office workers etc. in the background) are the only proletarians in the film.

Aside from cinematographer La Shelle's slow pan in the opening scene and a later graceful swoop in the Montagnino restaurant scene, there is very little attempt at adventurous camera improvisation. We remain at a safe medium distance most of the time. The only close-ups are of the detective's tautly thoughtful face and poetic shots of Laura.

The chief cinematic attraction lies in the characters themselves-- wry, sophisticated Lydecker, corrupt Shelby, the almost pathetic enamelled older beauty Anne Treadwell, the detective and the elusive Laura. Though each is sharply individuated, they also suggest classes or groups. On a certain subtextual level, then, *Laura* does express class consciousness.

Most of the action takes place in rooms like Waldo's--crowded with collectables. We move from Waldo's apartment to Anne Treadwell's and then to Laura's apartment. All three places look as if the same expensive interior decorator had a go at them. Even Laura's country cottage boasts the same fussy decor.

Other than these apartments, action takes place in an intime Italian restaurant, the dining room of the Algonquin Hotel, a cocktail lounge where Laura and her fiance Shelby Carpenter dance, unobtrusively watched by Waldo, and, very briefly, in an interrogation room at police headquarters. There is a claustral, cluttered feeling about these interiors.

There are only seven exterior scenes in the film. The first is Waldo and McPherson arriving in a cab at Anne Treadwell's building. It is daylight. In the second exterior scene, Waldo, Shelby and McPherson arrive in a cab at Laura's apartment. There is a crowd of gawkers and an ice cream truck outside. Daytime.

The third is Waldo's flashback account of his walk in the night snow outside Laura's apartment when he discovered that she was seeing the painter Jacoby. The fourth is McPherson walking in the night rain to Laura's apartment for another session of searching for clues. The fifth is Laura and Shelby talking in a car in the night rain. In the sixth Shelby drives in the night rain out to Laura's cottage. Finally, McPherson talks to a detective on night duty outside Laura's apartment just before the story's climax.

All these exterior scenes are brief and in uncomfortable summer sunshine, night rain and night snow. In the interiors, light comes into the room filtered through blinds or from frilly flounced lamps. There are constant references to the intense summer heat. In the novel we learn that it is August, 1941.

This is before the age of air conditioning. Hence Waldo is in his tub typing his eulogy for Laura and is able to observe McPherson looking at the antique clock and then reaching into the glass collection. "Careful," Waldo calls out. "That stuff is priceless."

Waldo, naked in his tub, receives the detective in the grand manner of a Roman emperor. Sitting in a tub of water to cool off was not an aberrant act in a Forties heat wave. People had oscillating fans, coffee shops had tall floor fans, some places had ceiling fans and none of the fans did much except make noise. Families slept out in public parks. Children ran through lawn sprinklers or opened fire hydrants. Lots of ice cream was consumed. Waldo sat in his tub.

Later, in his flashback story, Waldo will be seen again typing in his tub. He is typing a scathing attack on Jacoby. But the season is winter. Why sit in a bathtub to work if not for the purpose of cooling off? Waldo's habit of tub-sitting is as intriguing as Laura's choice to hang her own portrait over the mantel. Both actions hint at hidden psychological quirks of character. If Laura's act might be a symptom of self-love, Waldo's might be perceived as evidence of infantilism.

The novel makes frequent references to images of childishness. Both Waldo and Shelby often refer to Laura as a child. Bessie calls all of Laura's admirers (except McPherson) big babies or old women.

But aside from character development, the bathtub scene delivers exposition about Laura's murder, gives us a sample of Waldo's sharp wit and establishes McPherson as a hero who has a silver shinbone as souvenir of a shootout.

As Waldo dresses, McPherson asks more questions and plays with a toy baseball puzzle--one of those little glass-topped boxes with BB shot that must be rolled into slots. This toy appears several more times in the movie, once infuriating Waldo and another time mystifying Laura.

The toy may be the last vestige of a baseball metaphor from the novel. McPherson was initially annoyed at his assignment to the Laura Hunt case. He had planned to go to a baseball game that day and it was his day off. In his first visit to Laura's apartment he is puzzled by the presence of an autographed baseball on her desk. It does not fit with his conception of her as a pampered high society "dame." In all the extant scripts there is a scene in which McPherson forces Waldo and Shelby to go with him to the baseball game. The only baseball allusions that survive in the final film are McPherson puzzling for a moment over a baseball on Laura's desk and the toy, which, as McPherson says, keeps him calm.

Waldo accompanies McPherson to Anne Treadwell's apartment. Interrogation reveals that Anne has been lending Shelby a great deal of money. What kind of man borrows money from an older woman who is obviously smitten with him and who is his fiancée's aunt? Waldo calls Shelby a "male beauty in distress."

Shelby is, in fact, at Anne Treadwell's trying to escape reporters. Shelby offers as alibi a concert in the park. When McPherson asks what music was played Shelby says Brahms and Beethoven. Later on McPherson will reveal that this is a lie. A late program change made it an all Sibelius concert. Shelby says that he fell asleep and slept through the entire concert.

In the following scene, at Laura's apartment, McPherson will expose another lie: The key to Laura's cottage was not in the bedside table. Shelby put it there. But McPherson does not pursue either of these seemingly promising leads.

McPherson refuses Anne Treadwell's offer of a cigarette, but moments later lights one of his own. Everybody smokes. When we first saw McPherson at Waldo's apartment he was smoking. In Waldo's flashback account of how he first met Laura we see her smoking thoughtfully as he reads to her. We see Waldo throw his cigarette into the fireplace before he takes his winter night walk and discovers that Laura is seeing the painter Jacoby. When Laura first meets Shelby they have a cigarette out on Anne Treadwell's balcony. Smoking in Forties films was a multi-purpose device. Tough guys lit up. Lovers blew smoke at one another. Lighting a lady's cigarette was a courtship ritual.

The silver cigarette case Laura gave to Shelby was part of this courtship ritual. It was a costly gift, expressing her devotion and esteem. But because it is valuable Shelby obviously resented it. It was evidence of Laura's superior economic status. The act of giving it to Diane Redfern to pawn may indicate his resentment. In a parallel way McPherson's refusal of Anne Treadwell's cigarette is a cop ploy.

Waldo and Shelby accompany McPherson to Laura's apartment. Waldo reacts with anger when McPherson refers to Laura as a "dame." Waldo's attempt to justify and mythologize her is supported by the portrait and by a brief playing of her theme on the phonograph. McPherson seems at this point in the narrative to be unimpressed.

McPherson traps Shelby in a lie about not having a key to Laura's apartment. Then he stops a fight between Waldo and Shelby. The scene ends with Waldo bursting into anger at McPherson's baseball puzzle. "It's getting on my nerves," says Waldo. "I know," McPherson replies. "But it keeps me calm."

The following scene is in Montagnino's restaurant. A small orchestra is playing the Laura theme. McPherson and Waldo are at a table. Waldo is reminiscing about how he first met Laura. This was our table, he says. We dined here on her twenty-second birthday. But it was a different girl who had walked up to his luncheon table at the Algonquin Hotel five years earlier: A shy, frightened, breathless seventeen year old with an advertising portfolio under her arm. Coltish and seventeen. Waldo looks to be in his fifties.

The flashback continues with a montage of Laura's success in advertising and a growing friendship-romance between her and Waldo. But other men are attracted to her. First there is the painter Jacoby who did her portrait. Waldo demolished him with his weapons of wit and ridicule. There were others whom we do not see. And finally there is Shelby Carpenter, Waldo's most serious challenge. They meet at a party given by her aunt. Shelby gives Laura a rush full of humor, Southern gallantry and rueful self-deprecation. She offers him a job at her agency. Waldo is annoyed.

Waldo investigates Shelby's background and discovers lots of shadiness. People can change, Laura protests. Waldo counters with evidence that Shelby is seeing Diane Redfern. He offers the cigarette case which he redeemed as evidence.

Despite this clear proof of Shelby's deceit, Laura is still reluctant to break the engagement. The issue was undecided at the time of the murder.

A viewer might very well be puzzled by Waldo's possessiveness at this point in the film. What motivates him? When asked if he had been in love with Laura, he dodges and avoids an answer. There is of course his mentor role, his Pygmalion function. Laura embarking on a life of her own would disturb it. The average viewer might conclude that he *is*--or was--in love with her. But why not declare that love?

Vera Caspary did conceive of a very strong motive for Waldo's murderous possessiveness. This is why she was furious when she learned that her device of hiding the murder gun in Waldo's walking stick had been changed into a mundane shotgun. To her, the stick was a symbol of Waldo's impotent, frustrated love for Laura, twisted into destructive rage.

Waldo inadvertently reveals more than he prudently should in his flashback account. Since the flashback is laden with his own repressed love, and because one tends to over-eulogize the recently dead, Laura emerges in his story as a goddess, an iconic, transcendent figure. Definitely not a dame. And perhaps Waldo's story will have a strong effect on McPherson's emotions. Waldo may be helping create his most formidable rival.

A flashback in a Forties movie often provided an opportunity to express a mood of alienation. The events are in the past, done, final. Just this fact expresses a mood of fatalism and futility. A voiceover counter-pointed to a flashback could add a further irony. All this happened, the voice says and obviously I was powerless to change anything. Yet here it is, lived again.

In the following scene McPherson is on the phone in Laura's apartment talking to Mosconi's liquor store. He is holding a bottle of whisky. Had Miss Hunt ever bought Black Pony Scotch? Bessie enters and expresses anger because McPherson is reading Laura's letters and diary. She admits that she found the odd bottle--which had not been in Laura's liquor cabinet before Friday night--and two glasses in Laura's bedroom. She says with defiant pride that she washed the bottle and the two glasses off so that Laura's reputation would be shielded.

Shelby, Anne Treadwell and Waldo arrive. McPherson invites them to have a drink. He shows the bottle to each of them. None react. In the novel Shelby turned pale and was visibly shaken at the sight of the bottle. In the novel the whisky is Three Horses bourbon. In the scripts it became Black Pony Scotch. In the stage play it became Four Horses Scotch. There seems to be some indecision about how many animals and whether they are horses or ponies. Presumably a taste for bourbon reflects Shelby's Southern background. Black Pony Scotch is a cheaper brand than the liquor Laura habitually bought.

The next scene is McPherson alone in Laura's apartment. Outside it is raining. It is at night. McPherson is restless, prowling about, opening and closing desk drawers, looking at letters and diaries, opening and closing closet doors, drinking her good Scotch and looking at her portrait.

He has removed his coat and loosened his tie. This is as informal as anyone will get. Waldo put on a tweed suit after typing in his tub. Shelby is fully dressed in suit, shirt and tie when found at Anne Treadwell's even though he said that he had been lying down. Anne Treadwell looks too elegant for daytime. The formality of dress goes along with the expensive looking interiors. Laura's apartment is filled with mirrors. The style is art deco, but the plenitude of mirrors (along with the portrait) could also suggest narcissism. The mirrors might also suggest duplicity and illusion. When Laura first met Shelby she was looking into her compact mirror.

Everything in Laura's world is not what it seems to be. We first saw an enigmatic figure in a niche on Waldo's wall and a wall hung with masks. Waldo seems to be an elderly epicene wit. In fact he is a raging heterosexual who is capable of murdering a woman he cannot possess. Shelby the courtly Southern gentleman is a two-timing cadging leech, destined to be Anne Treadwell's gigolo. Diane Redfern is really Jennie Swoboda. And there is Laura. In back of the goddess on the wall is a real woman.

And even McPherson is not free from the web of duplicity. Outwardly a tough, unsentimental cop, he is inwardly a man capable of falling in love with a dead woman's image. Raksin's Laura theme is played in this scene on the lenatone (an instrument that made a piano echo with a shimmering vibrato,) and orchestra. The music emphasizes McPherson's emotional state.

The original function of the theme music was to offset audience anticipation of a different outcome to this scene. The conventions of a detective story call for murderers to return to the crime scene to retrieve a clue and then to hide when the detective arrives. Murderer then attacks detective and escapes. When a detective is alone in a house where a murder has been committed, audiences expect him to be attacked.

This was not going to happen in *Laura*. Therefore, to underscore a different plot direction (romantic) Raksin wrote the music.

McPherson opens the closet door and there are her dresses. Like Gatsby's shirts they express and embody success. McPherson reaches out a tentative hand to touch them. Impatiently he pulls his hand back and closes the door only to confront himself in the mirror that covers the door. He runs a hand through his hair. He does not like what he sees.

Besides narcissism mirrors suggest duplicity. The viewer sees himself and is thus in two places at the same time. This is not logically possible. Therefore, one of the two selves must be false. Or perhaps both selves inhabit one being and are only temporarily separated by the mirror. (i.e. films like *The Dark Mirror*)

The most well known use of mirrors to express ambiguity and duplicity is at the end of *The Lady From Shanghai*. Orson Welles confronts Everett Sloane and Rita Hayworth in an amusement park house of mirrors. Gunshots shatter image after replicated image. Illusion and reality are intermixed and confused.

McPherson falls asleep and Laura enters her apartment. She sees that the lights are on, comes in to confront an intruder sleeping in her living room. She threatens to call the police and a bewildered McPherson produces identification, saying "I am the police."

Laura had not seen a newspaper out in the country and her radio was not working. When the police had gone to her cottage she had been out walking.

"Better get out of those wet things," says McPherson. Laura looks a bit startled by solicitude coming from a policeman. As she goes off to change, a look of almost transcendent satisfaction or happiness flashes over the detective's face.

Laura returns with Diane Redfern's dress, found in her closet. Diane must have been the victim. McPherson begins to act like a suspicious detective. After all, if Laura is not a murder victim then she certainly must be added to the list of suspects.

McPherson leaves, asking her not to go out or tell anyone that she is alive. Whoever tried to kill her might certainly try again. Just before going, McPherson asks a hesitant question. Laura had gone to the country to decide whether or not to marry Shelby. What had she decided? When Laura says that she has decided not to, there is another flash of mingled relief, happiness on McPherson's face. It must be the swiftest suppressed smile in film history.

Up to this point in the story, a naive viewer, that is, one who had not read the novel--might have concluded that the detective's behavior was strange. He was obviously falling in love with a dead woman. The romantic or decadent attraction to death is not new in literature. But in the context of a conventional detective story one hardly expects to encounter La Belle Dame Sans Merci or Poe's Liegia.

McPherson's investigation has been a combination of shrewdness and seeming casualness. He caught Shelby in two lies and let him off the hook. He did not pursue the relationship between Shelby and Anne Treadwell. She is in love with Shelby and evidently keeping him. Therefore her motive for murdering her niece is strong. And McPherson does not pursue the bottle of Scotch matter.

The emotional flow of narrative in a detective story is both backwards and forward. Back in time to the crime and back beyond to the motives and forward to find the culprit. This flow became in many

Forties melodramas a drive not meant to end with disclosure, capture and closing the case. It became an inquiry into personality, into *who* more than whodunnit. The shift of focus in *Laura* is chiefly backwards. The detective is drawn into a preoccupation with finding out who the victim was. Given the predominately pessimistic view of women in Forties melodramas that kind of inquiry was safer when the subject was dead and thus historical. McPherson, we learned in the novel, read a lot of history.

The detective, like the historian or the biographer, has control over his subject. The murder victim can be photographed in the grotesque and awkward last pose. The detective can freely read her diary and letters, interrogate her friends and enemies. The victim can be wholly known.

An historian or biographer with a living subject must live in perpetual anxiety. Everything known can be negated in a few rash seconds. A dead subject is not given to impulsiveness.

Who was Laura? A two-timing dame killed by her cheap-bourbon drinking lover? A *real* lady as Bessie insists? Was she Shelby's "sweet child"? Waldo says she was a complicated modern woman. Now that she is alive, everything becomes speculative and open.

Laura's resurrection comes at an apt time in the story. McPherson's restless behavior can now be safely termed love interest and not a symptom of necrophilia.

When McPherson goes into the apartment building's basement to tell the policeman working on the phone tap to stop, the dial begins to click and both men overhear Laura calling Shelby who is not surprised to hear Laura's voice. Shelby asks her to meet him. "Dames," says McPherson. "Always pulling a fast one on you."

The two policeman split up to follow Laura and Shelby who have carried on a conversation in Shelby's car. McPherson follows Shelby out in the rain to Laura's cottage where Shelby retrieves a shotgun. McPherson confronts him and Shelby admits that he had taken Diane Redfern to Laura's apartment for a final confrontation. When the doorbell rang, Diane went to answer it. She was going to say that Laura had loaned her the apartment for the weekend. Wearing Laura's nightgown, in the shadowed entrance hall, the killer must have mistaken her for Laura and killed her.

Before leaving the cottage, McPherson turns on the radio. It works. McPherson is disappointed. He had hoped it wouldn't.

The next morning, McPherson comes to Laura's apartment with a bag of groceries. When he asks her why she broke her promise not to call anyone she says proudly that she never has done anything against her will. Bessie arrives and screams when she sees Laura. McPherson and Laura calm her down. Shelby arrives and he and Laura behave like a newly engaged couple. McPherson reacts angrily. Waldo arrives. Waldo collapses on seeing Laura. After giving him heart medicine, Shelby and McPherson carry him into the bedroom.

While Waldo is in the bedroom alone he calls all of Laura's friends and invites them to a "resurrection" party. While the guests mingle in the background (none ever become important enough to identify by name. Our attention is given solely to the five main characters, with some, to a lesser extent, to Bessie.) Laura learns from Shelby that he suspects her of committing the murder. Then she learns that her aunt is in love with Shelby. Anne also coolly says that she had thought about killing Laura but had not done it. McPherson receives a phone call and announces that he is bringing the murderer in. He looks grimly at Waldo and Shelby who clings to Anne's arm. Then he asks Laura to get her coat. Only Bessie reacts by screaming in horror. Laura thanks her, indicating that Bessie is the only person in the room who believes in her innocence.

As McPherson and Laura leave, Shelby takes McPherson's arm and McPherson punches him in the stomach. Shelby collapses onto a chair. Anne comforts him. This scene, and the climax are the only two violent physical actions in the film.

At the police station McPherson grills Laura under two intense bright lights. It is one step away from the old pre-Miranda days of the third degree. It is curious behavior coming from a man who has established himself in the audience's eye as a lover. Laura asks him to turn the lights off and he complies. He asks her why she is lying.

Why had she told him that the radio in the cottage was broken? She answers that she had left instructions at a local shop to have it fixed and left the key. Why did she say she had decided to break up with Shelby and then seemed to change her mind? Had she really decided to break with Shelby or did she say it because she knew that he, McPherson, wanted to hear it?

Laura reacts in surprise at the question. McPherson fumbles on. Then Laura admits that she lied to protect Shelby who looked guilty, but wasn't capable of murder. Do you love him? McPherson asks. "No," says Laura. "I don't know how I ever could have." A swift flash of relief and happiness comes over McPherson's face.

He ends the interrogation, saying that he had been ninety-nine percent sure of her innocence, but wanted others to believe that he suspected her. Also he had come to need the support of official surroundings. Laura smiles. It is a radiant smile of loving transport. The third degree has ended in a mutual awareness of love. McPherson takes her home and goes to Waldo's apartment. It is empty. As McPherson turns to leave, the clock chimes. He looks closely and intently at it. Then he probes for a hidden switch. Finding none, he kicks in the front panel revealing a hollow hiding space. It is empty. He looks thoughtful. Both he and we know that there is a matching clock in Laura's apartment.

Back at her apartment Waldo is warning Laura that McPherson is not to be trusted. He paces back and forth in anger. He pauses to look at the clock. McPherson arrives and tells Laura that her shotgun is not the murder weapon. Laura tells Waldo that his jealousy has spoiled her life--not, as he has posited, her weak judgment of men. She tells him to leave. He does, saying that he predicts a "disgustingly earthy relationship" for their future. "Listen to my broadcast tonight," he says. "It's on great lovers in history."

McPherson asks Laura if she knows how to open the clock's secret compartment. She says she doesn't and they both probe at it. The panel snaps open. Using a handkerchief, McPherson lifts a sawed-off shotgun out. Both barrels have been fired. It was Waldo, McPherson says. After Shelby ran from the entrance hall, he put the empty gun in the clock. "If he couldn't have you nobody else could."

McPherson leaves, telling Laura to "get some sleep" and "forget the whole thing like a bad dream." They exchange a chaste kiss. It is their only kiss in the entire film.

Meanwhile Waldo has been hiding on the stairs. McPherson asks the policeman on guard who is tailing Waldo? He hasn't come out the policeman says.

Laura is dreamily brushing her hair. The radio is on. Waldo's broadcast is ending. He recites Ernest Dowson's "Vita Summa Brevis":

> They are not long, the weeping and the laughter
>   Love and desire and hate:
>
> I think they have no portion in us after
>   we have passed the gate.
>
> They are not long, the days of wine and roses
>   Out of a misty dream
>
> Our path emerges for a while, then closes
>   Within a dream.[2]

---

[2] *The Poems of Ernest Dowson.* (London and New York: John Lane, The Bodley Head, 1905) p. 2. The poem was first printed in *Verses* (1896.) Since the poem does not appear in Dowson's manuscripts and was not previously published in a magazine before its inclusion in *Verses*, one might assume that it was written shortly before its publication. I do not know if Dowson was familiar with Poe's poem "A Dream Within a Dream," but some of Poe's lines are strikingly parallel:

> All that we see or seem
> Is but a dream within a dream...

The title is a quotation from Horace and means, in English: "Life's brief span forbids long enduring hope."

Dowson's poem (we only hear Waldo recite from the "days of wine and roses" line) is a perfect choice, a prime example of the Decadent movement, expressing a deep yearning for an end to desire and a yearning for death. There was no radio broadcast in Caspary's novel. But she later published a novel whose title alluded to the same poem: *The Weeping and the Laughter*.

As the last lines come over the radio we see Waldo slip in the back door and sneak over to the clock. The snap of the panel alerts Laura, but she does not investigate. Waldo takes out the shotgun, opens it and realizes that someone has taken out the spent shells. The look on his face tells us that he knows he has been found out. This does not stop him. He firmly inserts two new shells into the gun.

A radio announcer tells us that Waldo Lydecker has been heard through electrical transcription. The real Waldo stands next to Laura at her dressing table. She is intent on her mirror. "That's the way it is," says Waldo. He says that she has been the best part of him. He will not leave her to the "vulgar pawings of a second rate detective."

As the detectives pound at the doors, Waldo levels the gun. "He'll find us together as we always have been, as we always will be--"

Laura fends off the gun. One barrel goes off as she runs into the living room. McPherson bursts in the back door, takes her in his arms. The other detectives break in the second door as Waldo aims the gun, the policemen at the door shoot, Waldo staggers, the other barrel goes off. Waldo slumps, says "Goodbye, Laura...My love." And we see the clock's face, shattered by Waldo's shot. The theme music plays over fade to black.

What is the continuing attraction of this film? Placed next to *Double Indemnity* for example, we can see that *Laura* is not a *noir* movie. Laura is not a spider woman. Her elusive beauty elicits obsessive and destructive love from Waldo, but her feelings for him are limited to the loyalty one extends to a generous friend. She never meant consciously to lead him on. His obsessive and destructive desire to possess her is mainly sourced in his own twisted psyche.

McPherson's attraction to her is conventionally romantic, not decadent.

The film's mythopoic power is the result of several simultaneously coalescing elements. Foremost is the visual impact of Gene Tierney's beauty: lustrous eyes and lips, shimmering hair--all the code signals of Forties film beauty, with her own unique exotic quality added.

Secondly there is the aural effect of the music. As Elmer Bernstein put it "The mystique was supplied by the insistence of the haunting melody... We may not remember what Laura was like, but we never forget that she *was* the music."[1]

Johnny Mercer's lyrics support Raksin's haunting melodic quality and emphasize the out of reach dream-like generalized essence of Laura. Her unspecificity makes her Everywoman, or, rather, the woman of all men's dreams. Especially adolescent men:

> Laura is the face in the misty light
> Footsteps that you hear down the hall...

Thirdly there is the frame setting with supporting characters. It is an urbane, sophisticated setting, exhibiting good taste, clever wit and another ingredient so special to adolescent daydreaming--escape from the mundane. It is mainly Waldo who creates the air of sophistication. Some of his best lines came from the scripts, not Caspary's novel: Shelby as "a male beauty in distress," asking McPherson about the baseball puzzle "Something you confiscated in a raid on a kindergarten?" saying that he himelf wrote with a "goosequill dipped in venom."

"Laura," he says at Anne Treadwell's party, "I can't stand these morons any longer. If you don't come with me this instant I shall run amok."

---

[1] Roy M. Prendergast, *Film Music: A Neglected Art* (New York: Norton, 1977), p. 221.

"McPherson. . .It's a wonder you don't come here like a suitor, with roses and a box of candy (pause) drugstore candy of course."

"Haven't you heard of science's newest triumph--the doorbell?"

And his parting words to Laura and McPherson: "I hope you never regret what promises to be a disgustingly earthy relationship."

Of course these lines are enhanced by Clifton Webb's cultured, silky, deliberate and precise delivery, each phrase savored or bitten off as the mood called for it.

Finally, there is the fact that the film was released in wartime and is set in a time before the United States was at war. Both novel and film possessed a unique value for the wartime audience--an escape from the grim state of the real world into a realm of glamor and sophistication.

The attraction of nostalgia has built up with the passing of time. Although *Laura* has not attained the cult status of *Casablanca* or *The Maltese Falcon* it continues to hold a large and tenacious following. A 1987 catalogue of film memorabilia advertised a *Laura* poster for $325--the highest for any poster in the catalogue.

Laura has its own unique magic. But the record of how it got made is a complicated one, perhaps not different in essence from the way in which all films are made: a combination of accidents, timing, compromise, collaboration and luck--both good and bad.

Laura began its existence in Vera Caspary's imagination. It was an idea for a stage play which wasn't completed. Then it became a novel serialized in a magazine before it was bound as a book and advertised as a "psychothriller."

After that it went through various screenplay treatments and became the film. Only subsequent to that medium did it finally become a stage play and after *that* a television drama. Ironically it did not fare as well on stage as it did on film . Or the novel, which is an entirely different matter.

TWO: THE NOVEL

"The death of a beautiful woman is unquestionably the most poetical topic in the world."

--Edgar Allen Poe

Vera Caspary's novel *Laura* is about a beautiful woman of the same name who is murdered before the story begins.[1] She was shot in the face with a shotgun. Perpetrator unknown. Detective Mark McPherson is assigned to what he assumes will be a routine case and begins to interrogate her acquaintances. He starts with Waldo Lydecker, an Alexander Woollcott type columnist, who carries a great deal of gourmet weight, a Van Dyke beard, good taste in interior decoration, and a cane. Waldo claims to have discovered Laura and started her on her successful career in advertising as well as introduced her to good taste and his circle of sophisticates.

The first part of the novel is narrated by Waldo, who directs McPherson's suspicions towards Laura's fiancé, Shelby Carpenter, Southern aristocrat. McPherson questions Carpenter at Susan Treadwell's Apartment. Treadwell is Laura's aunt and obviously romantically interested in Shelby.

McPherson narrates the second part of the story. The routine case is beginning to become an ambiguous and complex matter. For one thing, his initial assumption was that Laura was just another "dame" who got involved with a lover who killed her. But the picture of her that is evolving from his probes into her past is different. She

---

[1] Vera Caspary, *Laura* (Boston: Houghton Mifflin, 1943). Subsequent references will be in parentheses in the text. The novel was originally serialized in *Colliers* Magazine (October-November, 1942) as *Ring Twice For Laura*. The *Colliers* title may be a half-allusion to James M. Cain's *The Postman Always Rings Twice* (1934). There have been three paperback editions: Popular Library in 1950, Dell in 1957 and Avon in 1970. At the time of this writing there is no paperback edition in print. A hardbound reprint of the first edition is available from Queens House/Focus Service in Dana Point, California.

was volatile, and complicated, capable of impulsive generosity and she was open and vulnerable. McPherson is beginning to fall in love with her lost image.

Then she comes back to life. Laura returns from a weekend in the country where she saw no newspaper. Her radio was broken so she heard no news. She had loaned the apartment to Diane Redfern, a model from her advertising agency. So it was Redfern who was shot, presumably by someone who assumed he was killing Laura.

McPherson leaves asking Laura not to let anyone know she is alive. Someone tried to kill you, he says, and they might try again.

Part Three is a transcript of a statement made by Shelby to McPherson on August 27, 1941. In Part Four, Laura takes over the narrator's task and Part Five, a kind of half climax, half epilogue, is narrated by McPherson.

The plot line of the novel is rather faithfully followed in the film with a few divergences. In the novel Waldo does not accompany McPherson to Sue Treadwell's. He only imagines what transpired there. "As narrator and interpreter," Waldo says, "I shall describe scenes which I never saw and record dialogues which I did not hear." (p. 11)

Shelby does not go with McPherson and Waldo to Laura's apartment. Instead, McPherson invites Waldo who goes reluctantly. There is, therefore, no search for Laura's cottage key and no confrontation between Shelby and Waldo at Laura's apartment. McPherson asks Waldo about the difference between Sibelius and Bach and therefore does not confront Shelby directly about his Friday night alibi.

The memorial service for Laura is omitted in the film. In the novel Bessie approaches McPherson at the service and volunteers the information about the bottle of bourbon. In the novel Shelby reacts vividly when shown the bottle. In the film he does not react. There is no interpolated story of Conrad told by Waldo in the film. In the novel McPherson does not prowl restlessly about Laura's apartment before her return. The interchange between Laura and McPherson after her return is much fuller in the novel:

> "Listen!" she said.
> We heard the sound of rain and the crackling of wood in the fireplace and foghorns on the East River.
> "We're in the midst of Manhattan and this is our private world," she said.
> I liked it. I didn't want the rain to stop or the sun to rise. . (p. 94)

The attraction between McPherson and Laura is developed more slowly and subtly in the film.

In the novel Laura lies about the bottle of bourbon to protect Shelby. In the film she reacts in bewilderment when asked about the bottle. McPherson questions Aunt Sue who tells him that Shelby had received a phone call in the middle of the night and gone out. Shelby comes in and tells them that he made a "sentimental journey" to Laura's cottage but did not go in. In the film McPherson hears the call on the tapped phone and follows Shelby out to the cottage where Shelby does go in to retrieve a shotgun. Much of the information Shelby gives in Part Three of the novel is related to McPherson in the cottage in the film.

In the novel Laura says she went to lunch with Diane Redfern on the Friday she went to the country. During lunch, Diane took out Shelby's cigarette case. In the film Waldo finds the case in a pawn shop where Diane had taken it. In the novel McPherson searches Diane's apartment, finds the cigarette case and afterwards confronts Shelby and Laura with it.

The changes from novel to film in general tighten up and speed plot movement. But the film's elimination of the three narrator structure makes amplification of character and motive more difficult to establish.

Through the prismatic viewpoint of the three narrators we learn that Waldo is possessive and domineering, Shelby is weak and treacherous, Susan Treadwell is vain and superficial and that Laura and McPherson are immediately attracted to one another. Lydecker is finally unmasked as the killer when he tries a second time to kill Laura with a shotgun hidden in his walking stick.

The multiple points of view also create a deliberate ambiguity. Caspary meshes a network of metaphor in the novel to support this ambiguity. We will encounter two mercury glass globes in the story. One is standing on Laura's mantel and the matching globe is in Waldo's apartment. The globes are referred to eight times, ending with Laura's globe shattered by Waldo's final shotgun blast. These globes are metaphors for the deceit and lies the detective must deal with in order to get at the truth. Things are distorted and refracted on the globe's surface. As Waldo put it:

> Glass, blown bubble thin, is coated on the inner surface with a layer of quicksilver so that it shines like a mirror. And just as the mercury in a thermometer reveals the body's temperature, so do the refractions in that discerning globe discover the fevers of temperament in those unfortunate visitors who, upon entering my drawing-room, are first glimpsed in its globular surfaces as deformed dwarfs. (p. 137).[5]

Each section of the novel is narrated in a style appropriate to the character speaking. Waldo's is fussy, cultured, literary and precious. Mark's is hardboiled yet sensitive. Laura's is intelligent and perceptive with a strain of persistent romanticism. Mark's interrogation of Shelby is dry and legalistic. It is an island of fact in the wash of ambiguity created by the subjectivity of three narrators.

One of the dominant networks of metaphor is art. Constant references are made to painting, theatre, film and literature. The art references, added to the subjectivity of the narrators contribute to the overall theme of shifting appearance and reality. The collision of two worlds--the detective's world of guns, gangsters and a rigid moral code

---

[5]Other references to this glass globe, which turns out to be a pivotal factor in solving the case, are on pp. 5, 39, 119, 138-9, 212, 226 and 235.

and a world of artifice, culture and refinement is complicated by the reader's growing awareness that the two worlds are much alike. Under the surface, the upper class world of antique collecting and taste is just as vicious and deadly as the detective's mean street.

And each narrator exhibits a flaw. Waldo's is his obsession with Laura and his frustrated knowledge that he can never possess her. Laura's is her "fatal weakness" for falling in love with the wrong kind of men. Mark's is his own penchant for romance. After all, it takes a special kind of person to fall in love with a dead girl's image on such short notice.

Waldo's style echoes Victorian stateliness. It implies a disdain for the modern age. It is ornate, elegant and pompous. Its wit is cruel and Wildean. There is a strong element of rhetorical posturing in it.

But Waldo's style reveals an essential shallowness. Often his wit is based on a mechanical reversal of old household maxims. "From trifling enmities do great adventures grow," he says (p. 6) playing a variation on the old great oaks from acorns cliché. He mentions Thackeray and O. Henry but the author he quotes from directly is Shakespeare.

He comments on McPherson's Cassius-like lean and hungry look. He quotes from *Twelfth Night:* "Concealment, like the worm i' the bud, fed on her damask cheek." (pp. 17-18) and from *The Merchant of Venice:* "Anyone who can't distinguish between Sibelius and Bach...is fit for treason, stratagem and spoils." (p. 46)

These are quotations a bright high school student would recognize. They border on cliché. His allusions to art--Dali, Eugene Speicher, Sargent--are also in the realm of the common. He quotes from his own work--his column *And More Anon* and books *February, Which Alone* (1936) and *Time, You Thief* (1938). The titles, with the appositions, are direct evidence of his late Victorian style.

His obvious fondness for popular culture exposes the essential middlebrow hiding behind the facade of high culture. He knows and loves the work of Noel Coward, George Gershwin, and Jerome Kern.

He has probably been to see Disney's *Bambi*. He recalls nostalgically that he took Laura on opening night to *Roberta*. "Smoke Gets In Your Eyes" is one of their favorite songs. *Roberta* was her first opening night and she reached out to take his hand. "Smoke Gets In Your Eyes," from that musical, is on Laura's phonograph.

There is a tendency in Waldo's style--and character--towards that element in Romanticism the critic Mario Praz identified as decadent in his study *The Romantic Agony*. Praz discussed, in the chapters "The Beauty of the Medusa" and "La Belle Dame Sans Merci" the Romantic's fascination with pleasure found in sadness, decay and gloom--especially when those emotions can be found in a a beautiful woman. The cult of "tainted" or cruel beauty ends logically in sado-masochism where pain and pleasure are equated.

Waldo's interpolated story of Conrad, the Amish youth who met a beautiful lady from the city and became obsessed with her is a striking example of this fascination with beauty and death. He begins with an old fashioned throat-clearing:

> "It is a legend told over port and cigars at Philadelphia dining tables some seventy-five years ago, and whispered in softer tones over tapestry frames and macramé work." (p. 77)

Conrad abandons his faith and his farm community to go off in search of the lady. A long time later he finally holds her in his arms and:

> "...the shadows, lilac tinted, in the shroud...
>
> Perhaps I neglected to mention that he had become apprenticed to an undertaker. And while the surgeon had declared her dead before Conrad was called to the dwelling, he afterward..." (p. 79)

Waldo hesitates, then fudges over the scene--leaving the necrophilia to complete itself in his listener's imagination. The audience is Mark McPherson and of course the subtext of Waldo's story of Conrad is that McPherson's love for Laura is sick. But much of Waldo's style reveals his own fondness for decay and death:

> Through the dusty wooden lattice and weary cotton vines we witnessed a battle between the hordes of angry clouds and a fierce copper moon. The leaves of the one living tree in the neighborhood, a skinny catalpa, hung like the black bones of skeleton hands, as dead as the cotton lilac. With the flavors of Montagnino's kitchen and the slum smells was mingled the sulphorous odor of the rising storm. (p. 66)

> Those millions of New Yorkers who, by need or preference, remain in town over a summer week-end had been crushed spiritless by humidity. Over the island hung a fog that smelled and felt like water in which too many soda-water glasses have been washed. (p. 3)

At the end of the novel we learn that Waldo planned a murder and his own suicide. There would be a final poisoned gourmet meal for both of them. When Laura broke their dinner date, he changed plans and used his shotgun instead.

Vera Caspary says that she meant the gun hidden in the walking stick to operate as a symbol of Waldo's impotence and frustration. It is an almost blatantly Freudian symbol.

Waldo himself draws attention to this tendency in the Romantic tradition:

> "The aristocratic tradition, my dear good friend, with its faint sweet odor of corruption. Romantics are children, they never grow up." (p. 134)

> "Have you ever analyzed that particular form of romanticism which burgeons on the dead, the lost, the doomed? Mary of the Wild Moor and Sweet Alice with Hair So Brown, their heroines are always dead or tubercular, death is the leit-motif of all their love songs. A most convenient rationale for the thriftiness of their passion toward living females." (p. 201)

Of course, Waldo projects the love of death on to Mark McPherson. He warns Laura that Mark needs to possess her, "possess, and revenge and destroy" her. (p. 202) He is actually talking about his own deadly obsession.

Mark McPherson's style of narration is firmly in the Hammett-Chandler hardboiled school. He uses Hemingwayesque short sentences and his metaphors are tough. Take, for example, his description of the scene at Montagnino's that Waldo termed *sulphorous*:

> The air was dead. Not a shirt-tail moved on the washlines of McDougal Street. The town smelled like rotten eggs. A thunderstorm was rolling in. (p. 84)

Waldo calls the air "sulphurous." McPherson says "rotten eggs." The Chandler style is persistent:

> Thunder crashed. It was followed by the stillness that precedes heavy rain. I was sweating and my head ached. I got myself a drink of water from the kitchen, took off my coat, opened my collar and stretched out in the long chair. The light hurt my eyes and I turned it off. I fell asleep before the storm broke...Thunder sounded like a squadron of bombers above the roof... (p. 85)

> The steel furniture in my bedroom reminded me of a dentist's office. (p. 84)

Passages like these would be at home in *The Big Sleep* or *The Maltese Falcon*. And McPherson adds his own unique social consciousness. He is no mere flatfoot. His reading taste runs towards the factual. He has read Gibbon, Prescott, Motley and Josephus's *History of the Jews*. His father used to quote Robert Ingersoll to him. He is very aware of injustices caused by a hierarchical class system. He expresses sympathy for the oppressed and makes ready identification with the maid Bessie's attitudes. There is, as Waldo points out, a strongly Puritan morality evident in his attitudes. McPherson agrees:

> This is my first experience with citizens who get their pictures into that part of the funny papers called the Society Section. Even professionally I've never been inside a night

club with leopard-skin covers on the chairs.... It takes a college education to teach a man that he can put on paper what he used to write on a fence. (pp. 83-4)

He describes Shelby "smiling at me like the King of England in a newsreel showing their majesties' visit to coal miners' huts." (p. 112)

When he searches Diane Redfern's apartment his sympathy with the proletariat is obvious:

> There were no bills as there had been in Laura's desk, for Diane came from the lower classes, she paid cash. The sum of it all was a shabby and shiftless life. Fancy perfume bottles, Kewpie dolls, and toy animals were all she brought home from expensive dinners and suppers in night spots. The letters from her family, plain working people who lived in Paterson, New Jersey, were written in night-school English and told about lay-offs and money troubles. (p. 115)

Buried in Mark's inventory of the things the girl brought home from her dates is a revulsion against the men who gave them. Men like Shelby who live off rich women and seduce younger ones with the rich women's money. Here, in Diane Redfern, is an explicit victim of the collision between the classes.

Laura shares Mark's class consciousness:

> My people were plain folk; the women went West with their men and none of them found gold; but Shelby came from "gentle" people; they had slaves to comb their hair and put on their shoes. A gentleman cannot see a lady work like a nigger; a gentleman opens the door and pulls out a lady's chair and brings a whore into her bedroom. (p. 178)

But Laura's class consciousness is complicated by the fact that she is now part of Shelby's and Waldo's world:

> I had met her (Bessie's) brothers, outspoken and opinionated workingmen whose black and white rules of virtue my intellectuals and advertising executives could never satisfy. (p. 187)

Laura faces the divisions and paradoxes in her nature honestly. She is realistic about her character complications. Yet she yearns for a traditional love relationship with a "real man." Through her narration the reader learns that she came to New York from Colorado Springs, Colorado, that she is hovering on the age of thirty, likes the music of Jerome Kern and is a baseball fan. A ball autographed by Cookie Lavagetto is in a prominent place on her desk. She reads Jonathan Swift. She has good taste in Scotch and has a quick temper. She conked Diane Redfern on the head with a trayful of *hors d' oeuvres* at a party.

"I had always been weak with a thirty-two year old baby," she says of her affair with Shelby. She is quick to share the blame for her "fatal weakness":

> The fault was mine more than Shelby's. I had used him as women use men to complete the design of a full life, playing at love for the gratification of my vanity, wearing him proudly as a successful prostitute wears her silver foxes to tell the world she owns a man. Going on thirty and unmarried, I had become alarmed. (p. 179)

"Like a gigolo seeking revenge against a fat old dowager with a jet band binding the wattles under her chin" (p. 174) Shelby revenged himself on Laura by his affair with Diane. Laura's clear view of her own emotional weakness is quite different from the view both Waldo and Shelby have of her. Waldo frequently calls her "child" and describes her as "Bambi's doe" when he recounts their first meeting. But in the opening words of her narration Laura reveals a capacity for tough self-awareness that is quite different:

> It's always when I start on a long journey or meet an exciting man or take a new job that I must sit for hours in a frenzy of recapitulation. (p. 167)

Later, Laura observes her neighborhood:

> Not one of my neighbors stays in town during the summer. There was only a cat, the thin homeless cat that nuzzles against my legs when I come home from work at night. The cat crossed the street daintily, pointing his feet like a ballet

dancer, lifting them high as if his feet were too good for the pavement. (p. 172)

Her metaphoric description of the cat echoes Eliot in "The Love Song of J. Alfred Prufrock" and resonates with Eliot's tone of urban isolation and loneliness.

The final effect of Caspary's prismatic narrational scheme--Waldo's fussy voice, Mark's tough guy voice and Laura's wistful realism--often relating the same scene again so that we perceive it in a new perspective--is deliberate ambiguity. Caspary uses persistently occuring metaphors of histrionics, art and illusion in her novel. Waldo looks like an epicene dandy. Laura's maid says he is an old woman. At one time McPherson saw him in a dim light in an antique shop looking like an old woman. He is no old woman. In fact he is a jealous murderer. Shelby is not the genteel Southern aristocrat but a leeching gigolo. Diane Redfern is really Jennie Swobodo. Aunt Sue is not a young desirable woman and she is no "auntie" type.

Only McPherson seems to be what he appears to be. Both Bessie and Laura refer to him as a man, "a real man."

Laura herself seems to be part of the network of duplicity. The art and histrionic metaphors adumbrate the initial key image in the film: her portrait. Instead of a warm-blooded human, capable of love and trust, we are given only the hard cold shaped surface of a work of art. Hence McPherson's hardboiled cop manner in his third degree interrogation of her. It is not her guilt or innocence that he wants to establish, but her essence. What kind of woman is she?

The theatrical metaphors begin with McPherson's initial meeting with Sue Treadwell and Shelby:

> The long mirror framed his (Mark's) first impression of Shelby Carpenter. Against the shrouded furniture, Shelby was like a brightly lithographed figure on the gaudy motion-picture poster decorating the sombre granite of an ancient opera house. (p. 24)
>
> In the mirror's gilt frame Mark saw the reflection of the advancing figure. . .As she paused in the door with the

marble statues and bronze figurines behind her, the gold
frame giving margins to the portrait, she was like a picture
done by one of Sargent's imitators...The rigid perfection of
her face was almost artificial, as if flesh-pink velvet were
drawn over an iron frame. (pp. 27-28)

As the scene goes on, it takes on a "theatric quality." Aunt Sue "cooed" "cried" "shrieked" and "declaimed." Shelby and Sue behave like actors on a stage. From this scene on, Shelby is always described in art or theatrical terms. When confronted by the bottle of Three Horses bourbon:

He was as harsh as metal, and his chiseled features, robbed
of color, had the marble virtue of a statue erected to the
honor of a dead Victorian. (p. 65)

This is Waldo's narration and he adds to the use of art images the device of the out of place; in particular Shelby looks like a figure on a motion-picture poster but the poster is on an old opera house. Aunt Sue looks like a painting done by an imitator. When he says that Jacoby, who did Laura's portrait, was an imitator of Eugene Speicher his comment is double barbed. Speicher was a popular portrait painter in the Thirties and Forties. He specialized in workmanlike studies of unsmiling women, usually seated, who looked aloof and haughty. Jacoby not only imitates. He imitates a minor second rate artist.

It is not only Waldo who indulges in art metaphor. McPherson describes Laura in a gold colored robe that made her "look like a saint on the window of the Catholic Church." (p. 89) McPherson says that Shelby sounds like words rolling off a sound track. The meeting between Shelby and Laura after she comes back to life is too perfect:

They embraced, kissed and clung. An actor after a dozen
rehearsals would have groped for his handkerchief in that
same dazed way. An actor would have held her at arm's
length, staring at her with that choir-boy look on his face.
(p. 122)

Waldo says, when he learns that Diane Redfern's real name was Jennie Swobodo and that prior to her modelling career she had worked in a mill in Jersey that it is like a bad novel. Laura herself comments on her relationship with Shelby that it "was like love in the movies, contrived and opportune." (p. 179) McPherson describes Waldo and Claudius, the antique dealer in terms of disguise and costume:

> The two men whispered. Waldo, with his thick body, his black hat and heavy stick, Claudius with his pear-shaped head, reminded me of old women like witches on Hallowe'en. (p. 139)

Men look like women, women are seen framed as in a painting, or in stained glass. Nothing is simply itself, all is distorted as if the whole story were reflected off of Waldo's glass globe.

The three styles come from disparate literary sources and interact to create the sense of clashing *milieux*. Waldo's wit and his allusions derive from the *fin de siècle*, Laura's is borrowed from romance fiction and the movies. McPherson's finds its antecedents in the hardboiled school of Raymond Chandler and Dashiell Hammett.

On the dust jacket of the first edition of *Laura* a sultry dark-haired woman's face is reflected in a globe. A cigarette has been left in an ashtray in front of the globe. Smoke rises in an art deco curve around the side of the globe. *A compelling novel* it says in quiet letters at the bottom of the cover, *of an impersonation undertaken in malice and completed in panic*. The back cover tells you all about the author and also asks you to buy war bonds.

On the cover of the Popular Library 1950 paperback edition of *Laura* a blonde woman in a black negligee, some cleavage, trace of belly button suggested and faint outline of thighs is looking wide-eyed and trying to move off the cover because there is a pistol pointed at her. We see a hand holding the pistol and a shirt cuff. That's all.

SHE WAS TOO BEAUTIFUL TO LIVE it says above the picture. There is a white dressing table behind her. There are pink knobs on the drawers, a pink ribbon on the lamp. The dressing table chair is flounced with lace. There is a pink ribbon on it.

Next to the woman's shoulder, which is bare because the negligee is negligent on that arm, it says LAURA HUNT EXERTED A FATAL FASCINATION OVER MEN. On the back cover it says A KILLER RINGS THE DOORBELL!! *He waits--and rings again. The door opens. She stands before him in a sheer negligee--*

In the novel's text, Laura's hair is described as dark. Once, Waldo commented on Laura's dark eyebrows caught by Jacoby in the painting. The murder was committed with a shotgun, not a pistol. We do not see the killing in the novel. It happened before the narration began.

Blonde women are ambivalent symbols in *noir* novels and films. There are the traditional "good" blonde women, like Alice Faye in *Fallen Angel* and there are the bad blondes, like Marilyn Monroe in *Asphalt Jungle*. Obviously the blonde woman on the 1950 *Laura* cover is sending ambivalent signals with all that white and pink decor and the sheer black negligee.

The typology goes back in literature at least to Scott's *Ivanhoe*. Rowena is the blonde Saxon girl from next door. Rebecca is the exotic, foreign (Jewish) woman. Rowena is insipid, but safe. Rebecca is tempting and sensual. Naturally, Ivanhoe prudently stays with Rowena.

The blurb on the first edition dust jacket said nothing. It was a marvel of intentional vagueness, perhaps appropriate for a mystery story with a surprise buried in it. The lurid breathlessness of the 1950 paperback is equally misleading, perhaps for more venal motives.

That black negligee with bare shoulder clashed with the wide-eyed fear, just as the white table with pink ribbons clashed with the blood red mouth. The cover is manifest of McPherson's perplexity. Is she a good girl, or is she, as Director Otto Preminger said flatly, a whore?

On the cover of the 1970 Avon paperback a woman with *dark* hair, looking like Gene Tierney, poses in a chair. She is wearing a blue demure robe which covers her everywhere. A chaste inch of white lace shows where the robe has parted, just below her neck. Her hands are delicate. The background is a deep red brocaded wallpaper. The border of the cover is a gilt frame. The cover is thus a framed portrait. *Laura* it says. *The story of a woman whose beauty could not die.* ONLY HER PORTRAIT REMAINED it says on the back cover.

Laura's image in these three editions of the novel has shifted from an enigmatic, difficult to see mystery woman, to temptress in black lace to the film-formed image of actress Gene Tierney exhibiting much good taste. A symbiotic relationship between the novel and the movie has existed ever since the film was released, but now the movie image dominates over the print medium.

While contemporary reviews of the novel were favorable, most of them referred to the dust jacket blurb which called the novel a "psychothriller." Obviously reviewers had difficulty coping with Caspary's uniqueness of genre.

The film eschews the novel's complexity. Except for Waldo's opening monologue, the three narrator device is dropped. An omniscient camera tells the story. Characters are simplified. Waldo the fat villain became Waldo the thin villain. Laura the complicated modern career woman became a remote icon, a dream object of desire. The film McPherson never admits to having read Gibbon or Swift.

The glass globe is eliminated. The gun is taken out of Waldo's stick and stuck in an antique clock. The criticism of social distinctions is muted. In fact, some scenes exhibit class-conscious snobbery: Bessie is patronized. Shelby swanks and swans about Anne Treadwell's kitchen staff. Bessie's Irish and McPherson's Scottish ancestry is eliminated. So is Laura's Colorado background. The network of duplicitous art metaphors is now only interior decoration.

The film has, of course, its own unique presentational force. The novel is unique on its own terms. It is an adroit mingling of a conventional detective story, a romance fiction, and is a study of frustrated, sadistic, obsessive love--a case history in morbid psychology. Unlike many murder stories which are devoured and put aside to be replaced by newer publications, *Laura* can be re-read with pleasure, because the emphasis is not mainly on *who* the culprit was but *why*.

THREE: PRODUCTION

> Laura is a mess. She is neither interesting nor attractive and I doubt if any first-rate actress would ever play her.
>
> --Darryl F. Zanuck's memo to Otto Preminger, Nov. 1, 1943.

Otto Preminger became interested in securing the film rights to Caspary's novel soon after its publication. At one point, he volunteered to collaborate with her on the stage version. Later he successfully campaigned to have Twentieth Century Fox buy the rights and the film was to be his debut as a producer.

Studio boss Darryl F. Zanuck told Preminger that he would never direct as long as he, Zanuck, ran things. Zanuck decided on a "B" budget for the picture. It was to be made cheaply and destined to be the bottom half of a double bill. Jay Dratler, a cultured and well-educated novelist, was given the task of writing the script. Lewis Milestone, John Brahm and Walter Lang all turned down the opportunity to direct. Rouben Mamoulian accepted and suggested Samuel Hoffenstein and Betty Reinhardt for a rewrite of Dratler's October 30, 1943 First Draft. Dratler's draft had already been rewritten twice by Ring Lardner Jr. The Hoffenstein-Reinhardt script was finished April 18, 1944. Some further retakes suggested by Zanuck after he saw the complete rough cut of the film were written by Jerome Cady.

John Hodiak was considered for McPherson, Laird Cregar and Monty Wooley were thought of for Waldo, Reginald Gardiner for Shelby and Jennifer Jones and Hedy Lamarr for Laura. Gene Tierney learned that Jennifer Jones had turned down the part and that may have soured her on the prospect of the role.[6] "Who wants to play a

---

[6]The studio was reported to have sued Miss Jones for the odd sum of $613,600.00 for the loss the company suffered, deprived of her Academy Award winning services in *Laura* (*New York Times*, May 14, 1944).

painting?" she said. However, the role was a chance to escape from the half-caste roles she seemed firmly trapped in. Apparently Mamoulian suggested Judith Anderson for Anne Treadwell. Zanuck replaced Mamoulian with Preminger.

Preminger pressed a case for Clifton Webb as Waldo. Zanuck was reluctant. He objected that Webb's experience was mainly on stage and that he was too obviously homosexual for the part. Zanuck asked for a screen test. Webb, who was at the time in a stage production of *Blithe Spirit* in Los Angeles refused to do a test. If Zanuck wanted to see him in action, he could come to the theatre. Preminger says that he resolved the situation by having his cameraman, Joseph La Shelle, go to the theatre to film Webb in a scene.[7] Zanuck was shown the scene, was impressed and agreed to the casting of Webb as Waldo. Joseph La Shelle says he has no memory of filming Webb in a theatre.[8] Whatever did happen, the film was finally cast. By this time, Zanuck was thinking of the project as an "A" budget picture.

There remained the question of music. Alfred Newman and Bernard Herrmann had both turned down the job. David Raksin got the assignment. Preminger had already tried to secure the rights for George Gershwin's "Summertime" but failed. He thought that the music used in the scene where the detective is alone in Laura's apartment might be Duke Ellington's "Sophisticated Lady."

At a meeting with Zanuck and Preminger, Raksin objected that the music would be wrong. "Sophisticated Lady" would imply to the audience that Laura was exactly that: a slinky, silky lady of the night. Also, would the music convey to the audience that the detective was falling in love with the murdered girl?

---

[7]Gerald Pratley, *The Cinema of Otto Preminger* (New York: Barnes, 1971), p. 58.

[8]Interview with Joseph La Shelle, August 20, 1984.

Preminger replied that Laura *was* a lady of the night. "She is a whore," Preminger said to Vera Caspary. "She has no sex. She keeps men. Gigolos."

Preminger's argument with Caspary was subsequent to the occasion with Raksin. He had given her a copy of the script to read and she was appalled at the changes. She objected to the loss of her important symbol of impotence--the gun in Waldo's walking stick. And she was troubled because Preminger obviously did not understand Laura's character. But Caspary's objections made no difference.

The Raksin-Preminger meeting was on a Friday. Preminger gave the composer the weekend to come up with a suitable alternative to "Sophisticated Lady." Raksin recalls that his heart was broken on Saturday, that he put off reading the letter from the woman he loved and who now wanted to leave him until Sunday and that after reading it, the opening phrase from the Laura theme came to him. By Monday morning the film had its score.

Raksin's score was unique in several ways. First of all, it was played over the credits and thus made an immediate and unforgettable connection between the visual image of Laura (the portrait) and the music. But the theme ceases as soon as action commences. After the use for credits, the Laura theme is not heard again until McPherson turns on Laura's phonograph and a few bars are heard. Then it is used more fully in the scene in Montagnino's restaurant, played by a small orchestra there. Finally it is heard in the night sequence for which it was written, using a shimmering piano (the "lenatone" which simulates vibrato with a mysterious sounding echo) against orchestra. As McPherson restlessly prowls Laura's apartment, obsessively returning to look again and again at the portrait, the theme music lets us know that he is falling in love with her image.

After the film's release the studio began receiving an impressive amount of mail inquiring about the music. Johnny Mercer wrote lyrics for it. In 1945 it was introduced on radio by Johnnie Johnston. Woody Herman's Columbia recording that same year sold over a million copies. It has since become the second most recorded popular song of all time. As of 1988 sixty different recordings have been done. Artists as diverse as Dave Brubeck, Rosemary Clooney, Errol Garner, Chris Conner, Dick Haymes, Charlie Parker, Stan Kenton, Paul Weston, Eddie Haywood, Pete Rugolo, Freddy Martin, Oscar Peterson, Jean Sablon and Cal Tjader have recorded it.

Yehudi Menuhin and Stephane Grappelli did a duo rendition and Joan Sutherland a solo. Spike Jones had his way with it. Frank Sinatra recorded it three times and has said that it is his favorite song. Cole Porter was once asked which song of all time not written by him he wished he had written and his answer was "Laura."

Jay Dratler's First Draft Continuity was completed on Oct. 30, 1943. A close reading of it reveals that Dratler was attempting to stay as close as possible to Caspary's novel in structure, character and theme. The opening scene, with Waldo's voiceover is a fair copy of the novel's opening paragraphs. The mercury-glass globe on a pedestal is singled out for close attention. The sun and sky over the apartment's terrace are reflected on the globe's surface. The globe is mentioned three times in the opening scene. McPherson is reaching for it when Waldo calls out his "Careful, young man" warning.

Dratler describes Waldo as middle-aged and bearded. McPherson "favors" his left leg. McPherson mentions the Dodgers-Boston baseball game and refers to Laura as a "dame." Waldo is annoyed. In the final film, Waldo flares up when McPherson refers to Laura as a dame when he enters Laura's apartment. In the final film, this is the first time that McPherson uses the term. Obviously Waldo's line "Will you *stop* (my emphasis) calling her a dame?" is a vestige left over from this earlier draft. In the final film, Waldo's melancholy voiceover ended with "another of those detectives" as the camera ends its sweep on McPherson. In Dratler's First Draft, the voiceover continues, in an obvious attempt to be faithful to Caspary's strategy.

In the final film, when McPherson and Waldo arrive at Anne Treadwell's and Shelby enters the room, one has the impression that he had arrived recently. In Dratler's Draft, Shelby arrived the previous night at 12:30 A.M.. This middle of the night arrival and staying all night reinforces the possibility of a physical relationship between Shelby and Anne.

When the three men leave Anne Treadwell's, they do not go to Laura's apartment as they do in the final film. Instead Dratler shows us McPherson forcing Shelby and Waldo to accompany him to the baseball game. The detective continues his interrogation as the game goes on.

Shelby gives his concert alibi and offers his ticket stub as evidence. Shelby says that he owns a shotgun but that it is in storage. He says that the key to Laura's cottage is at her apartment. At the end of the game, McPherson gives Shelby a baseball ticket so he can prove that he was at the game. Obviously this is meant to be a sly comment on Shelby's concert ticket stub alibi.

The baseball stadium scene is not in the final film, perhaps because it takes the action outside into the normal world and out of the artificial interior settings. McPherson's act of forcing Waldo and Shelby to accompany him--neither man is interested in the sport--could be (a) psychological pressure to test their alibis, (b) a kind of bullying sadism, or (c) both.

In Laura's apartment the record on the phonograph is "Smoke Gets In Your Eyes," another indication of Dratler's close adherence to Caspary's text.

At Montagnino's, Waldo points out carved initials in the table which he says was "our table." The initials are L.H and W.L. inside a carved heart. Waldo says Laura had carved it. Laura, in Waldo's flashback, shows more spunk in the Algonquin Hotel meeting than she does in the final film. Dratler shows a montage of Laura at work scenes, Laura at the hairdressers and in a dress shop (Waldo is in both of these scenes as a kind of Pygmalion figure), Laura and Waldo attending a first night at the theatre and going to the popular nightclubs of the era--Sardi's, the Stork Club, El Morroco. "Smoke

Gets in Your Eyes" is used to accompany this montage. Laura and Waldo are evidently involved in a romance in this draft.

A scene photographed but deleted from the final film shows a long banquet table set with crystal and flowers. Formally dressed men and women flank the table. They all have their heads turned towards the end of the table and have champagne glasses raised in preparation for a toast.

They are looking at Laura and Waldo who are standing at the end of the table facing one another. Is this an engagement party? The scene is not in this first draft although it could logically follow the courtship montage. Other scenes which were photographed but deleted include: Shelby, Waldo and McPherson at the ballpark. Shelby and McPherson are holding bottles of Coca-Cola. Waldo and Laura at the hairdressers, at a dressmakers, in a cab, dancing in a nightclub. Laura and Shelby in front of the Bullitt building. Shelby playing the piano.

When Waldo walks in the night snow outside Laura's apartment he discovers not Jacoby but Shelby there. Later, at Anne Treadwell's party, Laura pretends not to know Shelby. Now Waldo--and we--know that Laura can be deceitful. The ensuing scenes of Laura and Shelby's romance, as with Laura's and Waldo's, are more physically realistic than what remains in the final film.

When the two men leave Montagnino's McPherson takes over the voiceover narration. The device does help to make more explicit what he is thinking during his restless behavior alone in Laura's apartment. But in Dratler's draft, Laura does not return in this scene. McPherson alone and expressing uneasiness about his growing feeling for a dead woman is followed by a memorial service held at a funeral parlor. Shelby wears a black armband. Waldo comments caustically on commercialized grief. A crowd of gawkers rushes in and causes a ruckus.

McPherson returns to Laura's apartment. Waldo arrives and claims that the mercury glass globe is his. When McPherson refuses to give it to him, he threatens to smash it with his stick. This was an important clue in the novel: When Waldo destroys a glass globe in an antique shop McPherson gets an insight into a man willing to destroy a thing he cherished if he could not possess it. The incident in the draft, however, is not heightened.

After Waldo leaves, McPherson falls asleep and Laura returns. They seem instantly drawn to one another. McPherson's behavior makes this evident. And Laura's dialogue is mildly flirtatious.

Laura goes down to her janitor's apartment to see if her shotgun is in the storage room. She discovers the janitor's body. He has been murdered. She faints.

Later, McPherson forces Laura to come with him to tail Shelby out to the cottage. McPherson fluctuates between infatuation and suspicion. Shelby's phone number is found on a piece of paper in the janitor's apartment.

Now Laura takes over the narration. She tells McPherson that she loaned Diane Redfern the apartment. At her resurrection party Shelby confesses to her that he had been with Redfern on the night she was murdered. Laura reacts angrily. Art dealer Lancaster Corey tells Laura that McPherson had bid on her portrait during the time he thought she was dead. He also drops the information, off-hand, that mercury glass globes are weighted down with buckshot. Laura breaks her engagement to Shelby and tells everyone to go home. McPherson does not end the party scene, as he does in the film, by punching Shelby in the belly and taking Laura down to headquarters.

Post-party, Laura is alone. Waldo comes back. McPherson arrives. Waldo smashes McPherson's baseball puzzle with his stick. McPherson kisses Laura "brutally" in order to taunt Waldo, who leaves in a rage. Laura says sadly that Waldo got rid of every man she knew "just as surely as if he beat them to death with his stick." McPherson is startled by her words and reacts by rushing out.

Waldo is hiding on the staircase with his "ubiquitous walking stick." In the final scene a detective (not McPherson) punches Waldo, the gun in the walking stick shoots the mercury glass globe and Waldo is led off camera. McPherson and Laura embrace. End.

Aside from the baseball stadium scene and the murdered janitor, most of the plot incidents are taken directly from the novel.[9] Waldo narrates the first part of the story, McPherson the second and Laura the third. The characters, though less subtle than they are in the novel, seem realistic. Their desires and emotions are normal. Laura has verve and spirit. She is immediately and obviously attracted to McPherson. She is capable of carving initials onto a restaurant's table top. Laura carving initials is a rather implausible and out of character act. It is not, of course, in the novel.

The tabloid headline BACHELOR GIRL MURDERED. SEEK ROMEO IN EAST SIDE SLAYING is from the novel and emphasizes a sexual motive for the killing. It also gives some support to McPherson's early-on notion that Laura was a "dame." Shelby's arrival at Anne Treadwell's apartment at 12:30 AM and spending the rest of the night there makes their relationship more explicit.

But the progressive changes in Laura's character are the most striking in the transition from novel to draft. Her behavior with Waldo at their first meeting exhibits spirit and wit. Her subsequent relationship with him is obviously a romance as it is with Shelby and, presumably, the other men referred to. Certainly her girlish and flirtatious manner with McPherson is in keeping with the woman presented. We also learn from this draft that she is capable of deceit, can engage in sharp repartee and can lose her temper.

Changes made later exhibit a process of progressive derealization. She becomes more and more ethereal and out of reach, less and less a three dimensional woman with emotions and desires.

---

[9]The janitor's murder seems in retrospect to be a clumsy contrivance and was wisely dropped, along with Laura's memorial service mob scene and--thankfully--the carved heart and initials.

Perhaps making her more elusive and mysterious was to make the theme of obsessive love more evident.

Subsequent scripts also moved progressively away from the novel's themes and formal devices. Some of these changes may have been made in answer to the demands of the film medium. Voiceover narrators were common in Forties melodrama, but the use of three such narrators might have resulted in a clumsy effect.

Laura is sometimes referred to as a *noir* heroine. Fatal women were a staple of Forties noir movies. Barbara Stanwyck's Phyllis in *Double Indemnity*, Rita Hayworth's Elsa in *The Lady From Shanghai* and Linda Darnell's Netta in *Hangover Square* were sultry dangerous beauties who led obsessed men to doom. In *Woman in the Window* when Edward G. Robinson paused outside a shop window to look at a painting of Joan Bennett her reflection on the glass merged with the painted image. Robinson turned. Bennett was standing next to him. Robinson's troubles began.

Looking in a shop window in a movie is often a motif of psychological projection. The viewer sees his obsessions and desires objectified. And a portrait, like a mirror, is an equally powerful motif suggesting a double, or a confusion between appearance and reality.

Laura's status as noir figure is questionable. In this First Draft she emerges as a complicated romantic whose temperament often leads her into situations where *she* is manipulated and hurt, not the men she is involved with.

The fantasy women in Forties melodrama expressed a paradox. It was wartime. There was the girl back home and there was the girl picked up in a honky-tonk on shore leave. But maybe she was somebody else's girl back home.

Of course the virgin-whore axis is much older in the American mythos than Forties movies. But a number of factors combined in that decade to give the old fable a second turn of the screw. First there was the war itself as a fact--global and threatening to be endless, or at least lasting a long time. Propaganda permeated every aspect of home front life: newspapers, advertising, radio, songs and movies.

Coming from this fact was the need for morale boosting escape. Thirdly was the anticipated postwar brave new world. The concept of "wait for the bright tomorrow" includes the necessity of postponement, of putting off, of waiting as an act of patriotism. Propaganda created a kind of national psychic *coitus reservatus*.

Hence films that took one into another world. Back in time to London fog and gaslight or in a contemporary time but in a milieu unfamiliar to most of the middle class audience--perhaps a world of nightclubs and advertising executives and beautiful women and handsome men.

Mystery women in escapist movies in the early Forties were like pin-up pictures. They were attractive but unreal and out of reach. Laura is more a pin-up image (a demure one) than a fatal woman.

Dratler's Draft was a compromise among a number of forces. First was Caspary's novel. Dratler obviously attempted to be as close to it as possible. Secondly is the presentational demand of the film medium. Character's motives and behaviour cannot be too subtle. Dratler made them more realistic, and simpler. Thirdly were the conventions of the detective story and the romance genre. Dratler tried to satisfy both and ended up with carved initials, a fleshy relationship between Shelby and Anne Treadwell, a normal courtship between Waldo and Laura, and a murdered janitor.

And finally, Dratler could not have kept out the Forties psychic echoes if he had tried. And he evidently had not.

Dratler's Draft was rewritten several times and the Final Script was completed on April 18, 1944. Dratler retained credit as screenwriter with revision credit given to Ring Lardner Jr., Samuel Hoffenstein and Betty Reinhardt. A scene-by-scene analysis reveals post-Draft attempts to firm the characters and make the plot line simpler.

The opening shot is of a hot summer sky and an establishing shot of New York buildings: in the distance is a lone bus on Fifth Avenue. Waldo's voiceover accompanies these outdoor shots and continues for the inventory sweep of Waldo's exquisitely decorated apartment ending with "another of those detectives" as we see Mark McPherson regarding an antique French clock. The glass globe of both novel and First Draft has been changed to a clock.

Waldo warns McPherson not to touch the valuable glass collection and invites him into the bathroom where we and McPherson see Waldo naked in his tub, typing. The dialogue between the two men continues as Waldo gets dressed and then shifts to a taxicab en route to Anne Treadwell's apartment. McPherson admits that he is annoyed at having this routine case assigned to him because he had planned to go to the baseball game. The teams are changed from the First Draft. Instead of the Dodgers and Boston, now it is the New York Yankees against Philadelphia. In the novel, McPherson discovers a baseball autographed by Dodger Cookie Lavagetto on Laura's desk. Waldo protests that this is no routine case. McPherson answers that "some two-timing dame gets murdered in her flat practically every day." Waldo says angrily that Laura was no "dame." They arrive at Anne Treadwell's.

In the novel, most of this exchange takes place at Laura's apartment. There was no taxicab scene because Waldo did not accompany McPherson to Anne Treadwell's. McPherson never got to the ball game. In the final film the taxicab scene is truncated to a shot of it arriving at Anne Treadwell's building.

At Anne Treadwell's, McPherson questions her about her giving large sums of money to Shelby. Shelby enters the room. It appears that he has not been there very long. In the film he is fully dressed in suit, shirt and tie. Yet he says he has just been lying down. The suggestion of a physical relationship between him and Anne Treadwell established in the First Draft is toned down in the Final Script and film. In the novel, the relationship between Shelby and Laura's aunt

(Sue Treadwell in the novel) is much fuller: flattery, emotional game playing, theatrical posing and role-taking.

The three men leave and go to the baseball stadium. McPherson behaves alternately like a rabid fan and cop on the chase. He continues questioning Shelby, who is visibly uneasy. Waldo continues to make caustic comments which cast suspicion on Shelby. Waldo remains aloof and disinterested in the game. The three men leave after the seventh inning. McPherson presents Shelby with a ticket stub so he can prove he was at the game.

Since the baseball stadium sequence is not in the final film, the three men go directly to Laura's apartment after leaving Anne Treadwell's. Dialogue written for the stadium is shifted there. The elimination of the stadium scene does away with yet another outdoor setting, making the action in the final film increasingly claustral. But the deletion of the baseball game also deletes a promising plot line: the mutual interest in baseball could have added to the attraction between Laura and McPherson. In the final film, McPherson puzzles for a moment over a baseball found on Laura's desk, but says nothing.

The baseball game that McPherson didn't get to and the whole network of fan allusions are reduced to a toy McPherson plays with to calm his nerves. And dropping Laura's interest in baseball, like the deletion of her taste in literature, is part of the process of derealization.

At Laura's apartment, Shelby searches for the key to Laura's cottage which he plants and pretends to discover. McPherson confronts him with the deception and also reveals that the program at the concert had been changed at the last minute. McPherson does not follow up either lie. He and Waldo verbally duel over Laura's status as "dame." The record on the turntable has been changed from "Smoke Gets In Your Eyes" to the as yet unwritten theme music.

At the baseball game Shelby revealed that Laura had taken out a large insurance policy with him as beneficiary. When added to his lies and lack of alibi, one wonders why McPherson does not pursue him more vigorously. Obviously the subtext in the plot at this juncture is

McPherson's growing fascination with the personality of Laura rather than with who killed her.

The scene at Montagnino's restaurant is pretty much the same as in the First Draft, except that the initials and heart carved into the tabletop were put there by Waldo, not Laura. This is not much of an improvement, and the carved tabletop is wisely dropped from the final film. The account of the initial meeting between Laura and Waldo at the Algonquin is the same as the First Draft's. Laura is more spirited than she is in the final film in which she seems merely young and coltish. The Pygmalion montage is retained from the First Draft. In the film, however, only the scenes at Waldo's apartment in which he reads his column to her and prepares Caesar salad remain as evidence of any kind of romance between them.

Waldo's walk in the night snow ends with his discovery that she is seeing Jacoby, not Shelby as in the First Draft. Thus, evidence of Laura's capability for deceit is softened. The music played at Montagnino's is the theme, not "Smoke Gets In your Eyes." Waldo's savage attack on Jacoby in his column eliminates the man as a serious suitor, as it does in the final film.

Laura first meets Shelby at Anne Treadwell's party. Shelby is seated at the piano playing to a circle of admiring women. He asks Laura, who is passing by, what she would like him to sing. She says it does not matter. Her lack of interest shocks the other women whose attitude towards Shelby is described in the script as "Sinatraesque."

Darryl Zanuck suggested this scene as a means of establishing some reason for Laura's attraction to Shelby. He was to sing "You'll Never Know," a song made popular the previous year by Dick Haymes. The Decca record by Haymes sold over a million copies in 1943. The audience would therefore possibly recognize and respond to the song's romantic connotations.

No piano-playing scene in the final film. So we are left to speculate, as McPherson is, about just what attracts Laura to Shelby. As finally presented on screen, he is a glib smoothie with superficial charm--no woman as sophisticated and intelligent as Laura is supposed to be would be taken in by him.

The romance between Shelby and Laura is consistent with the First Draft's: as with the Laura-Waldo relationship, Laura and Shelby's is more physical than the final presentation on film. Waldo's discovery of the pawned cigarette case and Laura's subsequent trip to her cottage to think things over are retained from the First Draft.

As Waldo and McPherson part outside the restaurant, McPherson takes on the role of voiceover narrator. The next day, at Laura's apartment, McPherson calls Mosconi's liquor store to ask about the cheap brand of Scotch (Black Pony) found in the liquor cabinet. Bessie enters and the byplay between her and McPherson establishes that the Scotch had been there on Saturday morning, that she had wiped the fingerprints off and washed the two glasses she also found. Thus she protected Laura's reputation but aborted any chance of discovering who had been in the apartment on Friday night. McPherson does not pursue this line with Bessie. As with his puzzling failure to corner Shelby about his two lies, McPherson's apparent laxness with Bessie's evidence-tampering may be a symptom of his real attention being drawn elsewhere and away from the case.

He does try, however, to test his three suspects when they arrive and he invites them to have a drink and shows them the bottle. None of them react. In the novel, Shelby turned pale and looked faint.

The memorial service is dropped in the Final Script. We next see McPherson alone in Laura's apartment, restlessly pacing around and looking frustrated. His voiceover commentary on his feelings helps to establish that his emotions are in a turmoil. The voiceover also makes it evident that no murderer is to be expected lurking in a closet.

Waldo's arrival and attempt to retrieve the clock and his charge that McPherson's interest in Laura is sick and morbid interrupts McPherson's soliloquy. Waldo's imputation that McPherson's infatuation with Laura is necrophiliac loses much of its impact on the audience because they have been let in on the true nature of McPherson's confusion through his voiceover.

Laura's return and the events leading up to her meeting with McPherson are different from the First Draft's. In the Final Script she is less flirtatious, and Laura goes to her janitor's apartment so she can get into the storeroom to see if her shotgun is still there. The whole janitor murder episode is now dropped. McPherson forced Laura to accompany him when he followed Shelby out to the cottage in the First Draft. In the Final Script, McPherson goes alone. This change softens his First Draft harshness and hardboiled cop treatment of Laura.

Shelby confesses what really happened. The next day McPherson arrives at Laura's with groceries. Bessie arrives and screams. Shelby arrives and he and Laura act like lovebirds. McPherson reacts angrily. Waldo arrives and faints. Just as McPherson is about to arrest Shelby, Waldo, revived, enters and says he has invited all Laura's friends to a resurrection party. McPherson decides not to arrest Shelby. McPherson says grimly that *he* had already invited everybody.

There is a good deal more interchange between Laura and her friends than what was retained in the final film. Lancaster Corey tells McPherson that glass globes are often weighted with buckshot. Shelby tells Laura that he had gone out to her cottage to hide the shotgun. Laura reacts in shock. Obviously he believes her capable of murder. Laura and her aunt confront one another in the powder room. Anne reveals her true feelings for Shelby and admits that she had thought of killing Laura. After Anne leaves the room, Laura sits for a moment. It is obvious that she has sustained two psychic shocks: two people she believed loved her have betrayed her.

McPherson pretends to arrest Laura and takes her to the police station. Finally she admits that her attempts to cover for Shelby were in response to Waldo's attempts to make him look guilty. McPherson takes her back home. Waldo upbraids her for being attracted to McPherson. It is the same obvious pattern again. McPherson comes in. Laura turns on Waldo and sends him away. McPherson leaves.

Laura goes to the antique clock, fumbles with the panel at the bottom, finds the hidden spring, the panel opens to reveal a shotgun. Laura takes the shotgun out of the clock, goes out of her apartment and up the stairs to her storeroom where she puts the gun in a golf bag. Then she leaves and takes a cab to Waldo's.

Now the gun, hidden in Waldo's walking stick in both novel and First Draft, has been switched to the antique clock. And Laura's discovery of it and her act of hiding it can be read in two ways: she still has emotional ties to Waldo and is capable of covering up his crime and she is capable of deceiving McPherson.

Laura confronts Waldo with her knowledge. She begs him to run away. Waldo reacts in confusion, but admits that he had gone to get the gun and the rest of his memory is confused. Laura leaves. McPherson confronts her outside on the sidewalk. Roughly he puts her into a cab and tells a plainclothesman to take her home.

Meanwhile, Waldo is seen making a decision alone in his apartment. He leaves, and is seen going into Laura's storeroom, getting the gun out of the golf bag. There is a lot of stage madness business with Waldo fondling the gun "as if it were a living thing." Then he comes down the stairs and rings Laura's doorbell. He makes a speech about how she is the best part of himself and he will not leave her to McPherson's vulgar pawing.

As he aims, Laura covers her face. McPherson enters and grapples with Waldo. The gun goes off, shattering the clock. Waldo is subdued and taken away by detectives. Waldo's parting line refers to the promise of a "disgustingly earthy relationship." Fade to black.

A *final* final revision was done at Zanuck's insistence after he saw the uncut film. It was an *it was all a dream!* ending. This was shot and Zanuck sat through the movie again, this time in the company of his friend columnist Walter Winchell, who thought the new ending was implausible. Zanuck agreed and gave Preminger permission to re-insert the original ending.

Another rewritten scene leaves the golf bag episode out altogether, along with Laura's visit to Waldo's apartment. Instead, McPherson finds the gun in Laura's clock.

Laura says she suspected Waldo all along, but was reluctant to admit it since she owed him so much. She tells McPherson that Waldo's story of their Algonquin Hotel meeting was fiction. In reality she had lately arrived in New York, broke and was caught sleeping on a park bench. Booked for vagrancy, she was in night court when rescued by Waldo who was in court seeing low-life local color. He paid her fine and helped her find a job.

Like the carved initials, the night court story does not survive in the final film. A bad idea, as was "it was only a dream!"

FOUR: FINAL TAKE AND LAUNCH, OTHER VENUES AND SPINOFFS

Realities model themselves enthusiastically on one's desires.

--Stendhal

Laura in the novel is a complex character. She has had a number of love affairs that have failed. Her career, by contrast, is a success. Her taste runs from baseball and Jerome Kern to Jonathan Swift. In the First Draft much of this is dropped. She is still capable, however, of romantic sentiment. She carves Waldo's and her own initials onto "their" table. She has the normal flaws of the normal person. In the Final Script the flaws are softened. She gives less evidence of a capacity for deception. She does hide the murder weapon in her golf bag, but this is out of loyalty to an old friend.

But the woman encountered on screen would never have been arrested for sleeping on a park bench anymore than she would play golf or conk a tray over a rival's head or carve initials. Her dialogue is not swift and witty, her behavior with men is detached and aloof. She seems to move as if in a dream of her own making.

The changes made in Laura's character are as interesting as the ones made in the others. It is difficult to posit exactly how a film audience would have reacted to the Waldo Lydecker of the novel faithfully portrayed. Caspary's Waldo is fifty-two, six foot three inches tall, weighs over three hundred pounds, carries an antique walking stick, wears a Van Dyke beard, eyeglasses and a black homburg.

If Laird Cregar had, before his crash diet, played Waldo he would have come close to Caspary's character physically. But there are two immediately apparent problems any filmmaker would have had to confront. The first is the firmly established typecasting of fat men. They are either comic, as in the Oliver Hardy-Eugene Pallette line or evil in the Sidney Greenstreet-Francis L. Sullivan style. How would an audience react to Waldo, supposedly in love with Laura? They would find it difficult to accept a comic fat man in the role of obsessed lover. If they perceived the fat man as villain, then the murder mystery would be prematurely solved.

And Cregar had already established himself as a villain in *I Wake Up Screaming* and *This Gun For Hire*. In *I Wake Up Screaming* he played a murderer obsessively in love with his victim. In *This Gun For Hire* he was a peppermint eating dandy who betrays the killer he hired to do away with a blackmailer. A vicious person, but unable to kill petite Veronica Lake himself. He can't even order his chauffeur to do it. In an oily, squeamish way he says he doesn't want to hear the details, but we know he does. Cregar, if hitherto unknown to film audiences, would have made a fine Lydecker.

Waldo Lydecker is the fullest and most developed character in both novel and film. He has the best lines and the most interestingly complicated motivation. Clifton Webb's interpretation manages to be elegant without being epicene. His posture and walk are haughty and graceful. His timing and delivery wring every nuance out of the script. The thin Waldo is every bit as obsessed and driven as Caspary's fat man. Apart from the physical difference, the film Lydecker comes closer to the novel's intent than any of the other characters.

"The sexually unthreatening male," says Molly Haskell, "whether as romantic lover or friend, crops up repeatedly in fiction written by women." She goes on to elaborate:

> The character of Waldo Lydecker, the acid-tongued columnist, is a perfect example. In Preminger's cooly pervasive melodrama, the beautiful self-possessed heroine has evaded marriage largely through the ritual savaging of her beaux by Clifton Webb's brilliant Lydecker. They make a dazzling team--Gene Tierney's career woman and the epicene knife-blade lean New York intellectual. Lydecker has a hold on Laura that cannot be explained merely by her indebtedness to him.[10]

---

[10]Molly Haskell, *From Reverence to Rape* (New York: Holt, Rinehart & Winston), p. 167.

Yet Lydecker's "unthreatening" style is an elaborate mask that covers up heterosexual frustration and deadly rage. Lydecker has two weapons: his verbal wit and the gun in his cane. The wit is enough to do away with Jacoby. But it wasn't enough in Shelby's case.

And Laura's tenacious grip on Shelby is not in the pattern Haskell describes. Even after his initial betrayal with the cigarette case she does not break the engagement. It may be that she is approaching the symbolic age of thirty or that he simply looks good in public or that she harbors more romanticism than anyone suspects.

The case against Shelby is overwhelming. He lies about his affair with Diane Redfern, gives Diane the cigarette case, takes her to Laura's apartment for a tryst. Laura had loaned Diane her apartment, not her fiancée or her nightgown. But even in the face of all this deceit, Laura continues to help Shelby, pretending that their engagement is still intact in order to keep suspicion from him. All this is out of keeping with the self-controlled emotional game player outlined by Haskell.

The film's McPherson is a less complicated figure than Caspary's. In the novel, in his role as one of the three narrators, he reveals himself as sensitive, a secret romantic, intelligent, possessed of strong social opinions. He smokes a pipe, is a Brooklyn Dodgers fan and has a taste for reading history and biography. In the scripts he is converted into a typical tough cop. In the film Dana Andrews subtly suggests the romantic sensitivity without detracting from the tough cop characterization. But his ethnic background, his taste in books and his proletarian sympathies are not evident. He smokes cigarettes, presumably because a pipe is usually a thoughtful man's prop on screen. It is difficult to dangle a pipe at a hard guy's angle from the lip. Andrews copes with these changes however, and manages to suggest that less is more.

Andrews says that he had not read the novel and that, in fact, Preminger told him not to.[11] Perhaps Preminger did not want Andrews to confuse the diversified figure from the novel with the simplified cop of the film.

In detective films from the Forties on there has been a steady move towards a blurring of motivation between detective and criminal. The detective, as he gets closer to his prey, becomes emotionally involved with him, begins to identify with him, is forced to recognize elements in himself that he had always detested and fought against.

In order to cope with this confusion the detective often resorts to going outside the restrictions of the law by which he has always lived in order to confront and defeat the criminal. Or, contrawise, the detective may become obsessed with adherence to his code. Hence McPherson needing the comfort of offical surroundings and the machinery of the third degree in order to get at Laura's motivations.

McPherson had become as obsessed with Laura as her killer. Yet his code demands that she be included among the suspects after she comes back to life. Paradoxically, it is easier--or safer--to suspect a flesh and blood Laura. Before she was safely dead and an out of reach victim. A beautiful memory. Now she is real and may be a killer. A remote possibility. More likely she is a lady who is definitely not a dame who will walk him past furniture stores.

> "Sometimes I used to take my sisters' girl friends out. They never talked about anything except going steady and getting married. Always wanted to take you past furniture stores to show you the parlor suites. One of them almost hooked me." (p.38)

Laura's apartment is already over-furnished. Her life is full. Does she need a slightly used cop? Andrews conveys all this mess of emotion largely through physical nuance.

Laura is, of course, the most important character in the story. She is the center around which all the events revolve. First of all it is

---

[11] Letter from Dana Andrews (undated, 1984).

her supposed murder which draws all the other characters together. And she is the object of obsessive love--first from Waldo and then from McPherson. Finally, she is supposed to embody symbolic dream or fantasy powers. It is the idea of Laura, first projected by her portrait, then by her "story" or effect on others and ultimately by her actual presence that raises what might have been a routine detective story onto a mythopoeic level.

Gene Tierney manages to deal with all this rather well. Joseph La Shelle says that she was very easy to photograph. There were no bad or problem angles to deal with. She looked good in any light and she displayed great patience under La Shelle's painstaking to make each shot of her perfect.

In the Algonquin Hotel scene she is supposed to be seventeen, coltish and breathless with enthusiasm. Swiftly then she becomes the confident career woman with good taste in clothes and interior decoration. She is supposed to be real and yet at the same time able to convey an elusive, haunting mystery. Tierney delivers all of Laura's manifestations with poise and sureness.

Vincent Price's Shelby character does not leave him much room for elaboration. He is supposed to be a Southern gentleman whose facade of good breeding is flimsy. Even Laura sees through his pretenses. Shelby is supposed to be a shallow although charming leech. The excised piano playing scene might have added some dimension of charm, but there is little left for Price to do but stand around looking, as Waldo put it, like "a male beauty in distress."

So also with Anne Treadwell, a rich older woman who finds herself in rivalry with her own niece. Judith Anderson had specialized in malevolent women since she played Mrs. Danvers in *Rebecca*. But Anne Treadwell has little to do except look poised in the midst of her plush apartment and moon over Shelby.

Laura opened at the Roxy in New York in October, 1944. Hazel Scott and Jackie Miles were on stage. Reviews of the movie were generally favorable. *Variety* (Oct. 11, 1944) called it a "smart murder-mystery, expertly tailored in script, casting and direction." The review noted especially the "...deceptively leisurely pace at the start and its light careless air, only heightens the suspense without the audience being conscious of the buildup." Dana Andrews's performance was "intelligent" and "reticent." Judith Anderson brought "force" to her role and Gene Tierney was an "appealing figure."

The *New York Times* review (Oct. 12, 1944) was less impressed with Tierney. She was a "disappointment" who "plays at being a brilliant and sophisticated advertising executive with the wide-eyed innocence of a college junior." Clifton Webb and Dana Andrews were singled out for praise. Webb was "sophistry personified" and Andrews was shaping up to be a "sort of younger-edition Spencer Tracy" (p. 24).

Later in the month, Bosley Crowther did a brief feature on two new stars: Lauren Bacall and Clifton Webb. (*New York Times*, Oct. 22, 1944, Section Two, p. 1.) Crowther paid acknowledgment to Webb's distinguished stage career and said that on screen he was "polished, urbane and briskly trenchant." He plays a "creature of silky elegance whose caustic wit and cold refinements display him as a super-selfish man." His "fine hauteur and sleek intolerance expose him as a most successful snob." Crowther went on to say that the Lydecker character was a very unique and difficult kind of screen role. Crowther also noted the overall atmosphere of "refined decadence" in the film.

The movie was not a blockbuster, but it was well received. Obviously the studio found it difficult to find a way to publicize the film without giving away the "gimmick." Hence a lobby card is captioned *The story of a love that became the most fearful thing that ever happened to a woman.* A billboard announces: *When it came to men Laura gets by with MURDER!*

These were attempts to get people into the theatre, but perhaps the attempt to do so without giving away Laura's rebirth resulted in too much vagueness. When a stage production was finally mounted, the program lists Laura as "a girl" to avoid premature disclosure.

Perhaps the vagueness and ambiguity in the ads was unintentional, revealing difficulty in dealing with the meshing of genres.

A poster for *Laura* shows Gene Tierney looking straight ahead with no expression. Dana Andrews, wearing a hat, is profiled next to her, out of scale, obviously montaged there. He is looking in Tierney's general direction. An even smaller, out of scale Shelby, full figure is off to the right, holding a shotgun. He too is unconnected. The poster is vivid evidence that there was some confusion at the studio about what the film *meant*.

Laura received five Academy Award nominations. In that same year *Going My Way* and *Wilson* each received ten. Clifton Webb was nominated for Best Supporting Actor. Barry Fitzgerald won in that category for *Going My Way*. Webb won an Oscar for Best Supporting Actor two years later for his part in *The Razor's Edge*. He won a Best Actor Oscar in 1948 for *Sitting Pretty*.

Otto Preminger was nominated as Best Director and the team of Dratler, Hoffenstein and Reinhardt was nominated for the screenplay. But both of those Oscars went to *Going My Way*. Lyle Wheeler and Leland Fuller were nominated for Set Decoration but did not win. Of the five nominations, only Joseph La Shelle won for Best Black and White Cinematography.

Gene Tierney was not nominated and the *Laura* theme was not nominated. Tierney's only Oscar nomination in her career came the following year as Best Actress for her role in *Leave Her To Heaven*. (Now *there* is a real spider woman, a full-fledged *noir* harpy.) She lost to Joan Crawford.

Before *Laura* was in *Colliers* and before it was a novel and before it became a film, it was in Vera Caspary's imagination as a stage play. Sometime in 1940 she attempted to write the play. She abandoned the effort in Act Three. She had the basic situation of a woman shotgunned in the face and presumed dead and a detective who falls in love with her. But Caspary had not yet invented Waldo Lydecker, the man who kills what he cannot possess.

In the following two years the material became a novel. But even after the novel's publication and while film rights were pending, Caspary continued to pursue the idea of a stage version. She turned to George Sklar for collaboration. Marlene Dietrich expressed interest in playing the lead. It was not until 1945 that the Caspary-Sklar play was staged (without Marlene Dietrich.) In the play, the novel's action is truncated to fit three acts. Act One opens with McPherson seated in Laura's apartment, holding her portrait. Nineteen year old Danny Dorgan enters. He is the landlady's son. It is immediately evident that he had a crush on Laura. The character has obviously been created both to make Laura's mystique explicit and to forecast McPherson's own attraction to her. Waldo, Bessie and Shelby arrive in that order. Danny's mother enters. It is evident that she is domineering and possessive and therefore jealous of Laura. All of that adds up to another suspect with a motive.

Waldo and Shelby quarrel. Shelby leaves. Waldo and McPherson spar verbally. Waldo leaves and the scene ends with Laura's reappearance.

The bottle of whisky left in the apartment is renamed Four Horses and changed from bourbon to Scotch. Both Aunt Sue Treadwell and Anne Treadwell are eliminated. Shelby's concert alibi is retained. Waldo's globe is eliminated as is the film's French clock. Laura is given a sister instead of an aunt and the murdered girl's name is changed from Diane Redfern to Joyce Madden.

Scene Two of Act One is mostly interplay among Waldo, Laura and McPherson. The rivalry between the two men is more immediately evident than it is in both novel and film. Waldo shows the bottle of Four Horses Scotch. Bessie found it. Laura does not know where it came from. In the novel she pretended that she had bought it. Her lie was to cover up for Shelby. In the film it is a clue which leads nowhere.

In Act Two Danny Dorgan and Bessie enter and react strongly to Laura's rebirth. Shelby enters and his reunion with Laura seems deliberate and staged. Later on in the act, when they are alone Laura shows her anger over his deception. The bottle of Four Horses is her evidence. Shelby apologizes and tells her that he went to her cottage to hide her shotgun but was unable to do so because he discovered that he was being followed. The Act ends with McPherson receiving a phone call. The murder gun has been found.

In Act Three McPherson reveals that Laura's shotgun was not the murder weapon. Waldo warns Laura that she is committing the same fatal mistake: she is falling in love with McPherson who is unsuitable, just as Shelby was. Waldo accidentally on purpose breaks the vase with BB shot in it. Waldo reveals to Laura that he had intended to kill her. The doorbell rings and he escapes out the window. McPherson enters and goes out the window after Waldo. Laura is alone on the darkened stage. Waldo reappears. His walking stick hides a shotgun. As he is about to shoot Laura, McPherson fires from the window hitting Waldo in the hand. Waldo is led offstage by a detective. Laura and McPherson are left alone. Their eyes meet. Curtain.

A shawl, gift from Waldo to Laura, is introduced in the play. Laura never liked it. As Waldo is about to be led off to jail, he asks if he can have it. Laura says yes. The shawl, like the introduction of the Danny Dorgan character does little to advance the story. The play is a kind of merging, a distillation of both novel and film. The stage platform seems to demand further simplification. Waldo's and Shelby's character flaws are almost immediately evident. The attraction between Laura and McPherson is equally overt.

The play opened at the Q Theatre in London on January 30, 1945. Sonia Dresdel, a thirty-six year old English actress played Laura. The production was not successful. On April 19, 1946 an American production opened at the Playhouse Theatre in Wilmington, Delaware. Miriam Hopkins, then aged forty-four, played Laura. Tom Neal was cast as Mark McPherson and Otto Kruger portrayed Waldo Lydecker.

Reviewers agreed that Kruger was brilliant. He had a strong exit just before Hopkins's first entrance. The audience was still applauding him as she came on stage, thus lessening the impact of her ghostly appearance in a wet white raincoat. Some in the audience tittered.

Apparently the mixed reaction she received unnerved her. She demanded changes which involved firing the director, the lighting technician and the stage manager. The production moved on but not to Broadway.

On June 26, 1947 a recast *Laura* with Kruger again as Lydecker opened at the Cort Theatre in New York. K.T. Stevens played Laura and Hugh Marlowe was McPherson. Most of the critical reaction was negative, except for Kruger's performance and Stewart Chaney's stage setting. Brooks Atkinson said Stevens has beautiful hair but was a "coltish actress" who lacked poise. This production ran forty-four performances.

Twentieth-Century Fox telecast the play in a one-hour version on October 19, 1955. John Brahm (who had turned down a chance to direct the film) directed, Dana Wynter played Laura, Robert Stack did an Elliot Ness style McPherson and George Sanders was Waldo. Critical reaction was mixed. *Variety* said that Brahm's directing kept the story moving swiftly and smoothly. The one-hour telefilm was released in England as a film. British reviewers said it was routine melodrama with none of the gloss and atmosphere of the 1944 movie.

A color version was telecast on January 24, 1968 as an ABC Color Special. Truman Capote adapted this two hour version with Lee Bouvier as Laura, Farley Granger as Shelby, Arlene Francis as Anne Treadwell (the Treadwell character was not in the original Caspary-Sklar play), Robert Stack as the detective and George Sanders as Waldo.

Most of the advance publicity centered on Lee Bouvier, Jacqueline Kennedy's sister. Bouvier was making her dramatic debut.

Farley Granger said ". . .come next week she could be the laughing stock of the country."[12]

She was nervous and inept, which threw everyone else in the cast off. Critic Rex Reed called the production "one of the most agonizingly amateurish evenings TV ever produced." Another critic said, "A star is not born." *T.V. Guide* said "while she may be the worst actress let loose on an unsuspecting public since Toby Wing, Miss Radziwill (*i.e.* Bouvier) does photograph poorly."[13] On one aspect of the production, however, most critics agreed: David Raksin's theme music was the best part of the telecast.

Many of the reviews of these stage and television productions compared them--unfavorably--with the 1944 film. Some movies made subsequent to that film are obvious attempts to recapture the magic. If the stage and TV attempts were failures, the "tributes" and spinoffs also fall short.

Laura may echo some elements from Hitchcock's *Rebecca*. And it, in turn, may have set off resonances in Hitchcock's *Vertigo* (1958). Both McPherson in *Laura* and "Scottie" Ferguson in *Vertigo* are obsessed by women they believe to be dead but who are in fact alive. Both men are fascinated by portraits of their dream woman. Both men are Scottish, and hence are supposed to be hard-headed and anti-Romantic. There the parallels end. The woman in *Vertigo* is no saint. There is no Waldo figure and Scottie's attitude towards his reborn idol is brutal and sadistic.

Other films made after *Laura* attempted to use characters and themes from it as variations. In *Dark Corner* (1946) Clifton Webb plays a posh art dealer obsessively in love with his younger wife. He plans to murder her lover and frame a private detective (Mark Stevens) for the crime. Webb has a few Lydecker-style lines (i.e.: "I

---

[12]*T.V. Guide*, Jan. 6, 1968, p. 8.

[13]*T.V Guide*, Jan. 6, 1968, p. 8.

hate the way the lawn looks in the morning. It looks as if it was left out all night.") but the detective's love interest is in his loyal secretary (Lucille Ball.) Webb's wife (Constance Collier) is never presumed dead and hence is never reborn. She is not a remote icon of mysterious beauty. And she is not Gene Tierney.

In *Fallen Angel* (1945), directed by Otto Preminger, Dana Andrews falls in love with bad girl Linda Darnell (dark hair) but marries good girl Alice Faye (blonde, sings in the church choir) so he can kill her for her money. Andrews begins to fall in love with the good girl. Somebody murders the bad girl and Andrews is a suspect. The real killer is cop Charles Bickford, obsessively in love with Darnell. Bickford is no Lydecker. Musical score by David Raksin is not as memorable as the *Laura* theme.

In another Preminger film, *Where the Sidewalk Ends* (1950) Dana Andrews is a brutal street cop with a reputation for beating up suspects. Inadvertently he kills a man and then goes on a bogus hunt for the victim's murderer. The complication is that he falls in love with the victim's widow, Gene Tierney. No Raksin score, no Waldo Lydecker, the widow is no Laura and Mark McPherson wouldn't spend five minutes in the company of this rogue cop.

In *Leave Her to Heaven* (1945) Tierney played a wife so obsessively in love with her husband that she drowns his crippled younger brother, induces her own miscarriage and poisons herself to frame her husband so he'll be executed for her murder. If she can't have him...

In all of these attempts there are shreds and shards of *Laura* material--obsessive love, possessive and murderous love, duplicity, and appearance-reality duality. Is the beautiful woman also a good one? In some there is a juxtapostion of classes and in all there is a brooding mood of lurking evil. But the *Laura* mystique is not there. Gene Tierney was nominated for an Oscar for her role in *Leave Her to Heaven* but never repeated the mystique of her Laura portrayal.

Subsequent to *Laura,* to my way of thinking, Preminger never again achieved the same blend of glamour, romance, lurking evil, decadence and silky menace. Some of his films did deal with the theme of duplicity and obsessive love--*Angel Face, Fallen Angel, Where the Sidewalk Ends* and *Bunny Lake is Missing.* But others are nowhere near *Laura* in theme or style (i.e.: *Exodus.*)

Cinematographer Joseph La Shelle did some sixty movies after his *Laura* debut, was nominated for the cinematography Oscar for twelve of them (including *Hangover Square, Marty,* and *The Apartment*) but never received another award.

Other spinoffs might include *The Eyes of Laura Mars* (1978) in which Faye Dunaway plays a successful high fashion photographer surrounded by trendy friends who turn out to be toadies. Laura's posh admirers are revealed to be envious backbiting enemies or emotional leeches. There is one worshipful type from the lower orders--an ex-con as male Bessie. Laura is in danger. Her precognitive powers warn of murders. All the victims are people close to her.

Detective Tommy Lee Jones, from an antithetical milieu, hardboiled street cop, assigned to the case, falls in love with her. The feeling is mutual. Rene Auberjonois plays the epicene tart-tongued manager like a latter day Lydecker. There *are* overtones here. But there are also differences, the main one being that the detective turns out to be the killer.

But an attempt at a summarizing statement about the film-- beautiful career woman, surrounded by hypocritical friends, life in danger, the growing attraction between her and the cop from another world--sounds almost like a statement one might make about *Laura.* And in both films the beautiful woman is poised at the center of all the forces, object of desire and hate.

In a *Magnum P.I.* episode, Magnum is hired to investigate the murder of a successful young actress. She had been shotgunned in the face. Svengaliesque manager Ian McShane hires him. Magnum spends a night watching video tapes of the actress at work, like

McPherson restlessly working his way through Laura's letters and diaries or staring at her painted image.

Like McPherson, Magnum begins to fall in love with the murdered girl's image. Like McPherson Magnum finds that she is not dead after all. Someone else was killed by mistake. The killer (McShane) obsessed and jealous tries again and Magnum kills him. Being a weekly series, however, precluded anything permanent coming from the attraction between the detective and the mystery lady.

In *Sharkey's Machine* (1981), a beautiful call girl is shotgunned in the face. Detective Burt Reynolds had been keeping her under surveillance from a building across from hers. Obviously he was beginning to fall in love with her far off image. This being the Eighties, the image isn't in a gilt frame. The girl works out, plays tennis, sings along to "My Funny Valentine."

When the girl comes back, enters her apartment, she finds Reynolds asleep in a chair. She threatens to call the police. The incredulous detective recycles McPherson's gesture of taking out his shield and the line from *Laura* "I am the police."

In *Someone to Watch Over Me* (1987) a tough detective (Tom Berenger) is assigned to bodyguard an eyewitness to a murder. The witness (Mimi Rogers) lives in a posh apartment, listens to arias from *La Wally*, "Smoke Gets in Your Eyes" and, of course, Gershwin's "Someone to Watch Over Me." There is the inevitable attraction between the two people from clashing *milieux* with overtones of obsession. There is however no Waldo figure and the detective is married.

Laura was parodied on the Carol Burnett show (with Harvey Korman as Waldo and Steve Lawrence as McPherson) and in the novel *The Man With Bogart's Face*. A line from Laura was used as mood setting allusion in Elmore Leonard's novel *La Brava*: "Dames. Always pulling a fast one on you."

Shelby plays the piano and sings "You'll Never Know" at Anne Treadwell's party. Scene deleted from the film.
"LAURA" © Twentieth Century Fox Film Corporation. All rights reserved. 1944

A banquet hosted by or honoring Laura and/or Waldo. Scene deleted from the film.

"LAURA" © Twentieth Century Fox Film Corporation. All rights reserved. 1944

Waldo confronts Laura with proof of Shelby's philandering. Lobby Card.

"LAURA" © Twentieth Century Fox Film Corporation. All rights reserved. 1944

Advertising poster for Laura. The out-of-scale montaged figures indicate an attempt not to reveal the surprise twist in the plot: the victim isn't dead.

"LAURA" © Twentieth Century Fox Film Corporation. All rights reserved. 1944

CONCLUSION

> ...she is carved from Adam's rib,
> indestructible as legend, and no man
> will ever aim his malice with sufficient
> accuracy to destroy her.
>
> --Waldo Lydecker in Vera
> Caspary's *Laura*.

The attraction of *Laura* is due to some or all of the following elements:

1. The attraction of an unfamiliar world of danger which coexists with the safe and mundane (even boring) world we live in. In a film we can leave the world of everyday and enter--safely--the dark and dangerous place.

2. The beauty of the Medusa, Circe, and painted women under the gaslamps luring the farm boys. The women somebody warned you about (or should have) and to whom you are terribly attracted. Or, if you are a woman, the kind of woman it might be fun to be.

3. The myth of the fresh start. Starting over. Eyes across a crowded room. Searching for happiness. Taking off. Hitting the road. Can't repeat the past? Of course you can. Successful businesswoman falls in love with *real* man.

4. The clash of different worlds. Mean street meets uptown. The frisson of opposites attracted. In time this will be called "radical chic."

5. The love-death axis. Ode on a Grecian Urn. Still, silent, unmoving beauty outlasts flesh which is subject to the erosions of time.

6. Unconscious desires. Childhood fears. Images of sleep. Laura as Sleeping Beauty awakened by first kiss of true love. We, as children, knew that it would be a wonderful privilege to wake Sleeping Beauty, but what happens afterwards?

Film story begins with supposition. What if a man who owns a nightclub in Casablanca during World War Two runs into a former lover? *What if* is the beginning. But behind it are other concerns. John Ellis posits a concern behind the "what if" entrance:

> ...the relations between men and women, or more precisely, the problem of understanding the feminine, female sexuality, from a male perspective. Obsessively in classical narrative films, it is a woman who cannot be fitted in, who represents a problem or a threat to the male self- definitions and maculine positions.[14]

Edwin Panofsky has drawn attention to the psychological effects of viewing a film. The eye of the beholder takes in a series of visual images which are linked together in an uninterrupted flow of movement in space. The experience is akin to dreaming or hallucinating except that the viewer is awake and presumably in control of his mental faculties. As in a dream, psychological or symbolic content is experienced. But unlike a dream, where the content is personally and privately experienced, in film the content is directly projected on a screen.

It is this difference that makes film viewing a paradoxically involved and distanced experience. The real world is rendered almost tangible. Everything we hope--or fear--will happen. We viewers are like perceptive children observing the behavior of adults. We are outside the action but close enough to overhear and oversee action. When the action is forbidden or dangerous action, the film experience *is* childlike, furtive, voyeuristic.

This aspect of "dreaming while awake" becomes fantasy fulfillment, or vicarious satisfaction of certain primal desires in the film experience of *Laura*.

First of all, the detective, Mark McPherson is seen falling obsessively in love with a dead woman's image. Everything he knows about her is from secondhand sources: the idealized portrait painted by a man who had been in love with her when he did the painting (how

---

[14]John Ellis, *Visible Fictions: Cinema: Television: Video* (London: Routledge and Kegan Paul, 1982), p. 67.

true to reality *is* the image?) her possessions--furniture, books, dresses, perfume--the opinions of relatives and friends, and her letters and diaries.

Apart from pathological motives or the appeal of the decadent, McPherson's emotional frustration can be taken with sympathy. Or, the viewer, from his safe perspective can share the obsessive love. After all, it's only a movie. *We* aren't falling in love with a corpse.

Such an element is more at home in a vampire story or *fin de siècle* poetry. But it may also reach further back in our emotional history. It may be sourced in a fear of actual living women. They might make demands. An out-of-reach beauty hanging on the wall doesn't make demands. A fantasy woman conjured up from a whiff of perfume is unthreatening.

McPherson distrusts women. His relationships have been disappointing. When he takes over the Laura Hunt case he surmises that a "dame" has two-timed her lover. A "doll" once got a fox fur out of him. Evidence of greed, and calculation. A woman in his past kept walking him past furniture stores to look at parlor suites. Evidence of calculation. His words "doll" and "dame" are obvious attempts to trivialize women.

Perhaps Laura is different. McPherson yearns to believe it. But when he hears her call Shelby on the tapped telephone he reacts in disappointment: "Dames. Always pulling a switch on you."

When Laura is found not to be dead, McPherson's reaction is a curious blend of relief and suspicion. The man struggles with the cop. Perhaps the cop code is a way of keeping the living woman at a safe distance. Again, the film viewer is free to share McPherson's happiness over Laura's rebirth and join in the policeman's speculations about her true character. When Waldo later predicts that Laura and Mark's relationship will be "disgustingly earthy" his comment has some merit. What *do* the careerwoman and the street-wise gumshoe have in common? Will she go to the Policeman's Ball with him, sit beside him in the bleachers?

Waldo Lydecker's attitude towards Laura is equally bifurcated. First of all, he saw her as a beautiful object, like something in his collection of antiques. Moreover, he had a great deal to do with the creation of this particular objet d'art. So he has, in addition to the lust of the collector, the pride of the artificer. Beyond these attitudes we get into rather murky psychological territory. Is it simple physical lust? One problem with that is the difference in age. He looked to be in his late forties when they first met. She was seventeen. Waldo sometimes refers to himself as old. He calls himself "Old Mother Hubbard." Here we have a nuance of sexual confusion as well as age. Carpenter jokes about him dancing the polka. He also suffers from some sort of illness. When confronted with the reborn Laura he collapses and needs medication. Given all this, could he, realistically, be a serious suitor for Laura?

His flashback story shows Laura and he on one of their quiet evenings alone. He reads his columns to her. She listens eloquently, smoking thoughtfully. The audience would probably conclude that theirs is not a physical relationship. But earlier drafts of the script and some photographs of scenes shot but deleted from the final film show a more physical romance between them. Vera Caspary depicted Lydecker in her novel as an impotent man, driven to murder because of his frustrated love for Laura.

Certainly his ritual savaging of all Laura's potential lovers is evidence of *some* sort of strong emotion. And perhaps he keeps his real feelings hidden, mostly from detective McPherson, in order to divert suspicion from himself.

In the Hays Office, Johnson Office, Legion of Decency, Production Code days films were hampered in any attempt to portray certain aspects of human life (sexuality) realistically. Even married people on screen slept in separate beds. Movie makers resorted to a variety of code signals to convey sexuality to the audience. Gene Tierney's appearance was an almost definitive catalogue of most of those signals:

Shimmering, soft hair curving down to the shoulders, where it just coiled and lightly rested. One might imagine caressing that hair or *being* that hair touching the slender neck or shoulder. Soft shoulder. The hair almost, just almost touches the high cheekbones. Patrician cheekbones. Which accentuate the slightly slanted lustrous eyes. Exotic eyes, hinting of something Far Eastern, forbidden, mysterious. The wet, almost pouted lips.

Everything else was discreetly, modestly covered up. But we in the audience knew the truth. The hair, the eyes, the lips told us.

There is little physical action in *Laura*. McPherson stops a fight between Lydecker and Carpenter. McPherson punches Carpenter in the stomach at Laura's rebirth party. Lydecker tries to shoot Laura again, but she pushes the gun barrel away and the shot goes wild. McPherson and other policemen beat down her apartment doors. One of the policemen--not McPherson--shoots Lydecker.

That is all the physical action, aside from lighting cigarettes, walking in and out of rooms and talking. Most of the story is told through a series of set tableaux. Laura, in the second half of the movie, is usually in the center of these scenes. This keeps our attention on her, as her absence did in the first half of the film.

Taken as a whole, the novel *Laura* is a more complete work of art than the film. The characters are more three-dimensional, the three-person narration creates a *Rashomon*-style complexity and the psychological motivation makes the novel stand out above most routine mystery stories.

Laura is a more complex and intersting person in the novel than she is on screen, where most of her action is *in*action. Obese Waldo Lydecker reveals more cruelty and perversity than the screen's slim villain. Mark McPherson is allowed to be more complicated in the novel too. The fact that he is capable of falling in love with a phantasm has more authenticity as a result.

The multiple narrators also allow for three different styles, each one revealing aspects of the narrator's character. Lydecker's is witty but cruel and perhaps subtly shallow with echoes of obsolete rhetoric. Laura's is sensitive and perceptive. McPherson's is basically hardboiled, in the Chandler-Hammett line, but also revealing sensitivity and a social conscience.

Much of this is deleted from the film's characters. A study of the various scripts reveals a process of derealization and simplification. Yet, despite the novel's evident edge in fictional sophistication, the film has outlasted it in both popular and critical reputation. What are the reasons for the movie version continuing to fascinate and draw attention?

Laura has been called a classic of *cinema noir*. When one outlines the main characteristics of *cinema noir*, the conclusion fits uneasily if at all.

In *noir* films danger awaits the unwary and unlucky man. Usually he is entrapped by lust and/or greed. Often these two are combined. For example, Walter Neff in *Double Indemnity*. Neff, a respectable insurance agent, is attracted to Phyllis Dietrichson but suspects that she wants to murder her husband, make it look like an accident, and collect the insurance. Neff refuses to discuss a policy with her and beats a hasty exit. But he knows that his escape is momentary. He really cannot help but get involved. Events take a grim, fatal course and the story ends with the guilty lovers shooting one another.

The danger often is masked by a facade of wealth, elegance and sophistication. Duplicity and a confusion between reality and appearance often take the form of oblique plots, devious story-lines.

Sometimes the chief metaphor for this confusion is a mirror. (i.e.: the house of mirrors in *The Lady From Shanghai*.)

The settings in *noir* are predominately urban. The city is seen as a concrete jungle, as a dark labyrinth:

> Like the western and the gangster film, *noir* uses the same kind of settings over and over. Night clubs, hotels, tenements, police stations, offices, docks, factories, warehouses, crumbling mansions, boxing arenas, train stations, restaurants both shabby and luxurious are as integral a part of *noir* as private eye and two-timing dames. Like the great city itself, individual locations are charged with menace.[15]

Character is as formalized as setting. *Noir* abounds with psychopaths, sadists, victims, detectives (often *private* detectives, in order to underscore their isolation) and spider women. "I'm backed into a dark corner," says Mark Stevens in *The Dark Corner*, "and I don't know who's hitting me." This line sums up *noir* sensibility: hidden menace, helplessness and a sense of fatalism.

Sometimes there is a clash of *milieux* and character in *noir*. Sophisticated uptown meets grim downtown. Evil lurks in both. "Sophisticated" takes on the connotation of decadence.

How does *Laura* qualify as a *noir* classic? It is a murder story set in a city. The victim is a beautiful woman. There is a tough detective. The settings are a world of elegance, wealth and taste. But soon we perceive that the settings are duplicitous. Things are not as they appear. The beautiful woman's adoring fiancé is a liar, a cheat, possibly a thief, certainly a gigolo. The woman's devoted aunt is in reality a jealous rival. Her best friend and mentor turns out to be the one who tried to shoot her.

But the victim is not a man, as the unlucky and unwary victims in *noir* usually are. Whatever the motive for her killing, it does not

---

[15]Foster Hirsch, *The Dark Side of the Screen: Film Noir* (New York: A.S. Barnes, 1981), p. 85.

appear to be caused by her own greed or lust. Moreover, the victim is not really dead. Someone else was killed in her place. Now she, returned to life, joins the list of suspects.

And the detective is not a private eye. He works for the police department. He doesn't have a shabby office with a bottle in the bottom desk drawer and a faithful secretary in the reception room.

However, the world of *Laura* is a dangerously deceptive one. Part of the danger is the fact of the yet uncaught killer, capable of firing a double barreled shotgun into a woman's face. Part of it is a psychological duplicity. The detective is frustrated when faced with the enigma of Laura. How is it possible for someone so perfect to remain faithful to the obviously corrupt Shelby? As McPherson put it: "...for a charming intelligent girl you've certainly surrounded yourself with a remarkable collection of dopes." Trying to fathom Laura's character becomes, for McPherson, as urgent a problem as unmasking the killer.

For the film viewer, this entrée to a dangerous world and into the confusing set of conflicting emotional motives is, as all fictional experiences are, an escape into another, alternative, possible world. The audience can, when the show is over, return to its mundane--even boring--but safe world.

But the audience cannot say with critical exactitude that what has been experienced in *Laura* was a *noir* film. Perhaps part of the reason for its *noir* reputation was the studio advertising which tried to keep the surprise rebirth of the victim a secret. The result was a confused and confusing message (i.e.: "Laura Got Away With Murder!")

Of course the 1944 audience did not know that it was viewing a classic, *noir* or otherwise. Back then a film was merely devoured, absorbed and supplanted by other films.

Beauty is dangerous. Everybody knows that. Ezra Pound's Hugh Selwyn Mauberly "observed the beauty of Circe's hair" rather than "the mottoes on sundials" and thus condemmed himself to the status of minor artist. Even Robert Frost felt that the attraction of "lovely, dark and deep" woods on a snowy evening might lead to the eternal sleep of death.

St. Thomas Aquinas defined The Beautiful as having three essential qualities: wholeness, harmony and radiance. A thing which is complete in itself, lacks defects, pleases the eye because of its harmonious proportions and draws attention to itself because of its inner effulgence, can be called beautiful.

But there is another theory of The Beautiful at odds with the Thomistic position. The attraction of the morbid, the decayed, the grotesque and dark. Some find aesthetic pleasure in the contemplation of decrepit ruins, in things sick, dying or dead.

If the beautiful can be aligned so readily with either good or evil, obviously the contemplation of a beautiful thing is a dangerous activity. Laura's beauty is first perceived in her portrait. The painting itself is an object of attention and desire. McPherson tries to buy it. This is before he meets the flesh and blood woman. In Caspary's novel, Laura's character is known prismatically. Both Lydecker and Carpenter often refer to her as a "child," a "poor child" or a "dear child." Obviously this is an attempt to make her more helpless and vulnerable (and, perhaps, less threatening) than she reveals herself to be in her share of the novel's narration.

McPherson's account of his attraction to her is, in the novel, more evidently normal. It is only Lydecker who insists that McPherson's interest is pathological, necrophilic. This, of course, may be projection on Lydecker's part.

On screen a lot of the complications in her character are deleted. She is as beautiful as the portrait, but almost as iconic and out of reach. The beauty of Circe, Laura's portrait and pin-up pictures have the advantage of being unreal. They are objects which can be freely fantasized about. In *Brute Force* (1948) each of a prison cell's inmates uses the same pin-up picture as a means of engaging in a daydream about real women in their individual past lives. The picture is actually an artist's idealized composite of the movie's female stars: Ella Raines, Yvonne De Carlo, and Ann Blyth. Like the painting of Laura, *Brute Force*'s pin-up picture presents an aesthetic alternative to reality.

"A photograph," says Diane Arbus, "is a secret about a secret." Walker Evans's *Atlanta, Georgia* (1936) shows movie billboards juxtaposed to decaying buildings. An ironic reading of this photograph would make the contrast between glossy false dreams and grim reality. Yet a neutral iconographic interpretation is also possible. The gentrified structures *and* the billboards are both caught in time. Both are subject to decay. One can see peeled and weathered bits of older posters on the board to the right of the big poster for *Love Before Breakfast* (starring Carole Lombard.) *Love Before Breakfast* will fray and decay and be peeled off in time to be replaced by other posters for newer movies.

Glamor photographs are obviously artifice. Everyone knows that a studio glossy has been retouched and airbrushed, that adroit lighting has enhanced good points and eradicated bad ones. Natural defects have been removed and what is left is dead perfection. This knowledge does not spoil our pleasure. Knowing that the portrait of Laura is a studio glossy of Gene Tierney, blownup and brushed over to give it the effect of paint does not spoil our appreciation of it. Keats said it in "Ode on a Grecian Urn." Dead perfection is superior to living passion, which is caught in time. The portrait's final effect is romantic, idealized, derealized. Unlike *Atlanta, Georgia* the portrait of Laura is timeless.

The attractions of fantasy and the advantage it holds over reality are especially appealing to the adolescent. Adolescence is a time of doubts, fears and powerful desires. There are violent mood-swings between confidence and despair. There is half-baked rebelliousness, grandstanding, giving in to whim, harboring resentment, sulking.

And there is over-dependence on the opinions of others and adherence to a rigid code of what the world should be. Small wonder that the adolescent seeks relief in daydream or fantasy.

Fantasy in *Laura* can possibly be seen in a number of what Kristin Thompson calls "dream cues" in the dialogue. "Get some sleep. Forget the whole thing like a bad dream," McPherson says to Laura. Darryl Zanuck suggested an "it was all a dream!" ending for the film. It was scripted, shot and discarded. Thompson suggests that vestiges of sleep and dream remain in the final film. In fact she posits a theory that the entire second half of the movie, from the time McPherson falls asleep in Laura's apartment on could be read as one long dream sequence. Many forties movies used dream narrative. We have the example of *Woman in the Window* for instance. Almost the entire film is Edward G. Robinson's dream.

David Raksin's music helps to underscore the dream element in the film. And afterwards, Mercer's lyrics reinforce Laura's dream quality. As Mercer put it in the song's verse:

> You know the feeling
> Of something half remembered
> Of something that never happened
> Yet you recall it well...

The yearning of the youth trapped in adolescence *and* the middle class and living in someplace not particularly interesting for something more is mythic. Read Thomas Wolfe. If one lived in a tame suburb, then trips to the city were both dangerous and exciting. To see the powerful and beautiful and elegant people sharing the sidewalk was to bring dreams of fulfillment very close. To think *someday* and then go home to the drab ordinary. Or to sit in the popcorn dark and see the dreams unveiled, projected, palpable. As Bruno Bettelheim put it:

> As an adolescent I went to the movies as often as I could and for the same reasons as young people do today: I needed images I could emulate in forming my personality, and I was eager to learn about those aspects of life and adulthood

which were still hidden from me. Moving pictures, more than any other art, give the illusion that it is permitted to spy upon the life of others, which is exactly what children and adolescents do, in order to find out how these adults manage their lives, and even more important, how they manage to satisfy their desires...[16]

In Carlos Fuentes's novel *Holy Place*, an aging movie star is asked to define a good film. "It's the one the spectator thinks he dreamed when he's leaving the theatre," is her answer.

"On the surface," Eugene Archer says, "*Laura* is an ultra sophisticated 'whodunnit' making a mystery not only of the killer but of the corpse. The face of the beautiful victim, staring from the shadows of an elegant portrait, dominates the audience as thoroughly as it motivates the characters involved in her demise; for that face has been destroyed, before the film begins, by a blast from a doublebarreled shotgun." --Laura had inhabited a "rich and rigid circle of poised, impeccably mannered sophisticates, gliding from their Madison Avenue advertising agencies to antique-furnished penthouses and Connecticut cottages designed by Frank Lloyd Wright."---seen through the detective's eyes, Laura "is the eternal myth of womanhood-- a shimmering, exquisite creature of beauty and Mystery, incisive intelligence and maidenly warmth, a dream goddess coveted by a privileged universe --she is mercurially fascinating and infinitely unreal."[17]

"...Watching the movies," says Bruno Bettlelheim, "Carried me away so that I was no longer quite myself.... I was lifted out of my shell into a world where what I felt and did no longer had any relation to the real me or to reality."[18]

---

[16]*Hollywood: Legend and Reality*, ed. Michael Webb, (Boston: Little, Brown, 1986), p. 17.

[17]Eugene Archer, "Laura" *Movie*, 2. (Sept. 1962):12-13.

[18]Webb, *op. cit.*

Movies, and indeed, any fictional experience has this power to take us out of ourselves. Fiction provides us with a repertoire of false memories that exist side by side with real ones. Children learn to fantasize, invent and pretend. They explore and probe into reality with their toys and thus gain dominion over unfamiliar territory. So do adults.

Movies bestow omnipotence and, sometimes, omniscience. We are privy to scenes between characters that other characters in the story know nothing about. We know that Waldo Lydecker has entered Laura's apartment by the rear door. Laura is listening to his radio broadcast. We know that it is a recording. McPherson asks the policemen on duty about Lydecker leaving the building. We know he had not. For the time that we are watching the film, we are in a superior position to everyone in it.

Moreover, films help us to avoid mortality. Either a sad or happy ending has the same aesthetic result: after all, it's only a movie. Unlike the ragged edges of our own lives, the incompleteness, the failures or successes that all exist in a temporal continuum that can only have one ending, our own, film story has satisfying psychological limits and a sense of proportion and order.

Alexis de Tocqueville and Frederick Jackson Turner, commentators on American life and character, have pointed out a spirit of restlessness, a love of innovation and unflagging optimism in the American character. Turner found its source in the physical presence of a frontier over a long period of time. Up until 1893, when the U.S. Census Bureau declared that there was no longer a frontier, there always had been one. It was in a number of different geographic locations and it kept moving steadily westward. But there it was, a place one could point to and believe that things were not settled, locked in, finished. An individual could fail back east and start over on the frontier. Turner hypothesized that this factor kept American civilization open-ended and young. After the physical fact of a frontier was over, the concept became myth.

Consider the Western novel and movie. Consider country-western music with its emphasis on loneliness, heartbreak and starting over again. Consider *The Great Gatsby* with its romantic hero who believed in the American myth of the fresh start. He believed in the self-made man, and created a totally new personality for himself. He believed in the everlasting power of first love.

The fact that his vast wealth is due to illegal activities is irrelevant. The wealth itself is irrelevant. It is what can be done *through* the wealth: create a place where he and his first love Daisy can relive the past. Gatsby embodies a deeply entrenched belief.

The year after *Laura*, Joan Crawford won a Best Actress Oscar for *Mildred Pierce*. Crawford played a middleclass housewife who began selling homemade pies to restaurants and became a rich woman in a big fur coat. Like Gatsby, all her efforts were for love. Mildred Pierce's love was lavished on her daughter, who turned out to be as unworthy as Daisy.

Caspary's Laura was the veteran of a number of unsuccessful love affairs. She rationalized that her continuing though unhappy attachment to Shelby is in part the panic of growing older and still not married and partly due to vanity: Shelby looks good in public. This aspect of her past is eradicated in the film. We know, specifically, only about Jacoby who painted her portrait. There were others, Lydecker says, but they weren't important. Until Shelby. He was a problem that would not go away.

If Waldo had not tried to kill Laura and she had returned from the country determined to marry Shelby, what would ensue? Possibly Waldo would try again to kill her, possibly succeed. If not, then the Hunt-Carpenter marriage would probably not end well. Shelby's character is set: resentment, theft, unfaithfulness, lying. Not much there for a stable future.

For Laura, being out of town while someone else was killed by mistake was a stroke of luck. How else would she ever get to meet Mark McPherson? A real man. A baseball fan. A real second chance. Laura, like all good Americans, believes in the second chance.

And there is the interesting mix of two worlds. This was a popular theme in movies from the Thirties on. Usually it was material for comedy, as in for example *Designing Woman* (1957). Lauren Bacall, successful dress designer, meets and falls in love with sportswriter Gregory Peck. Each finds the other's world hard to take.

Caspary's Laura had Colorado farm roots and was a baseball fan. The film excises much of this. We see her in flashback at the beginning of her career and in flashback montage style we see her swiftly moving up in that career. Therefore, with no evidence to the contrary, she seems very much at home in Lydecker's values. But we have also seen McPherson's contempt for Lydecker's world. What will McPherson offer to Laura in its place? Laura does not know. But she has faith in the fresh start. In starting life over again.

Besides the increasing simplification of Laura's character in the various stages of the script, McPherson's character is also simplified. Lydecker is the most complete, the most complex member of the cast. Some secondary characters--Detectives McAvity and Schultz and art dealer Lancaster Corey--are all but written out and become all but invisible. Even Shelby Carpenter and Anne Treadwell are peripheral. Bessie, the maid, is little more than a swiftly sketched stereotype.

Our attention is thus forced into a narrow perspective on the two men and Laura. The two men have relevance and interest *because* they are rivals over Laura. The vanishing point perspective zeroes in on Laura herself.

Today's films are the inheritors of all film history as well as works that have their own context. The museum scene in *Dressed to Kill* (1980) is a frame-by-frame recapitulation of the museum scene in *Vertigo*. There is a stalking in a hall of mirrors scene in *Someone to Watch Over Me* that is obviously an allusion to the hall of mirrors scene in *The Lady From Shanghai* as well as, perhaps, a reference to the mirror motif in *Laura*.

But the mirror motif reaches even further back in the narrative tradition to the Medusa who cannot be faced directly. To the mirror in Cocteau's *Orpheus* that the poet passes through in order to reach the underworld. Perhaps the pool of Narcissus is the first mirror in which the ego finds itself loved and in stasis. Love, and especially self-love, leads to the death of the self.

Contemporary allusive use of *Laura* material contains elements that could not have been in the original work. The obsessive object of the detective's love in *Sharkey's Machine* is a call girl. Sex attraction *and* consummation are realistically rendered in contemporary movies.

However, in *Someone to Watch Over Me* the detective is able to break out of his bewitched trance and return to his middleclass wife (who looks pretty good too *and* can give the family car a tune up.) Realism has more than a sexual face.

In David Lynch's 1990 television series *Twin Peaks* the continuing mystery was "who killed Laura Palmer?" The girl is dead before the series begins. The plot includes a parakeet named Waldo and a veterinarian named Lydecker.

These tributes are variations on a theme. The mythic figure remains intact. A truer representation of Laura, more faithful than the adaptations or the painting behind the credits, would be a hologram. A figure deeply embedded in some clear medium, like lucite. Then she would be seemingly three-dimensional and simultaneously evoke a feeling that the perceived woman is not real and is out of reach.

It is this quality of *almost* that invests the Laura image. Almost real, almost tangible, almost ethereal. Her claim on our imagination is set forever in flickering black and white and in the musical signature. It is there and can be rewound and unreeled again and again.

BIBLIOGRAPHY

Andrews, Dana. Letter to author. 24 Jan. 1985.

Archer, Eugene. "Laura" *Movie*. 2. (Sept. 1962): 12-13.

Arhheim, Rudolf. *Film as Art*. Berkeley, Calif.: University of California Press, 1966.

"As We See It." *T.V. Guide*. 17 Feb. 1968: 1.

Behlmer, Rudy. *America's Favorite Movies: Behind the Scenes*. NY: Ungar, 1982.

Beja, Morris. *Film and Literature*. NY: Longman, 1979.

Belton, John. *Cinema Stylists*. NJ: Metuchen, 1983.

Berger, John. *Ways of Seeing*. NY: Viking, 1973.

Bettleheim, Bruno. *Hollywood: Legend and Reality*. Ed. J. Michael Webb. Boston: Little, Brown, 1986.

Bogdanovich, Peter. "Bogdanovich Interviews Otto Preminger." *On Film*. 1. 1 (1971): 37-52.

Bordwell, David. *Narration in the Fiction Film*. Madison: University of Wisconsin Press, 1985.

Branigan, Edward. "Formal Permutations of the Point-of-View Shot." *Screen* 16. 3. (Autumn, 1975): 54-64.

_____. *Point of View in the Cinema*. Amsterdam: Mouton, 1984.

Caspary, Vera. *Laura*. Boston: Houghton, Mifflin, 1943.

_____. and George Sklar. *Laura: A Play in Three Acts*. NY: Dramatists Play Services, 1945.

_____. "Mark McPherson." Ed. O.M. Penzler. *The Great Detectives*. Boston: Little, Brown, 1978.

_____. "My *Laura* and Otto's." *Saturday Review*. 26 June 1971: 36-37.

_____. "Ring Twice for Laura." *Colliers*. Oct. 1.7, 24, 31, 1942. Nov. 7, 14, 21, 28, 1942.

_____. *The Secrets of Grown-ups.* NY: McGraw Hill, 1979.

Cohen, Mitchell S. "Villains and Victims." *Film Comment.* Nov.-Dec. 1974: 27-29.

Crowther, Bosley. "Two New Stars: Lauren Bacall and Clifton Webb." *New York Times Book Review.* 22 Oct. 1944. Sec. 1: 1.

Dowson, Ernest. *The Poems of Ernest Dowson.* London and New York: The Bodley Head, 1905.

Dratler, Jay. *Laura.* First Draft Continuity Screenplay. Microfilm. 30 Oct. 1943.

_____. and Samuel Hoffenstein, Betty Reinhardt. Additional scenes by Ring Lardner Jr. *Laura.* Shooting Final Script. 18 April 1944.

Durgnat, Raymond. *Films and Feelings.* Cambridge, Mass: MIT Press, 1971.

_____. "Paint it Black: The Family Tree of the Film Noir." *Cinema* (Uk) No. 6-7. Aug. 1970: 49-56.

Ellis, John. *Visible Fictions: Cinema: Television: Video.* London: Routledge and Kegan Paul, 1982.

Evans, Mark. *Soundtrack: The Music of the Movies.* NY: Hopkinson and Blake, 1975.

Hansen, Miriam. "Pleasure, Ambivalence, Identification: Valentino and Female Spectatorship." *Cinema Journal* 25. 4. (Summer, 1966): 6-32.

Haskell, Molly. *From Reverence to Rape.* NY: Holt, Rinehart and Winston, 1974.

Hirsch, Foster. *The Dark Side of the Screen: Film Noir.* NY: Barnes, 1981.

Hopper, Hedda. Column Interview with Clifton Webb. *Los Angeles Times.* 4 May 1944: 36.

Kracouer, Siegfried. *Theory of Film: The Redemption of Physical Reality.* NY: Oxford University Press, 1965.

La Shelle, Joseph. Personal interview. 20 Aug. 1984.

Lourcelle, Jacques. "*Laura*: Senario d' un scenario." *L'avant Scene Cinema.* 212. (July-Sept. 1978): 5-11.

Maltin, Leonard. *The Art of the Cinematographer.* NY: Dover, 1978.

McConnell, Frank. *Storytelling and Mythmaking.* NY: Oxford University Press, 1979.

McVay, Doug. "Faithful in His Fashion: Otto Preminger's *Laura.*" *Bright Lights.* 8. (1979): 26-36.

Mulvey, Laura. "Visual Pleasure and Narrative Cinema." *Screen.* 16. 3. (Autumn, 1975): 12-20.

Murray, Edward. *The Cinematic Imagination: Writers and the Motion Pictures.* NY: Ungar, 1972.

Musel, Robert. "The Princess and the Play." *T.V. Guide.* 6 Jan. 1968: 4-8.

Panofsky, Erwin. "Style and Medium in the Motion Pictures." *Critique.* 1. 3. (Jan.-Feb. 1947): 5-28.

Peary, Danny. *Cult Movies.* NY: Delacorte, 1981.

Place, Jane A. and L.S. Peterson. "Some Visual Motifs of Film Noir." *Film Comment.* Jan.-Feb. 1974: 30-32.

Porter, Dennis. *The Pursuit of Crime: Art and Ideology in Detective Fiction.* New Haven: Yale University Press, 1981.

Pratley, Gerald. *The Cinema of Otto Preminger.* NY: Barnes, 1971.

Preminger, Otto. *Preminger: An Autobiography.* NY: Doubleday, 1977.

Prendergast, Roy M. *Film Music: A Neglected Art.* NY: Norton, 1977.

Raksin, David. Recording liner notes. *David Raksin Conducts His Great Film Scores.* RCA ARLI-1490. 1976.

_____. Personal interview. 14 Aug. 1984.

Schrader, Paul. "Notes on Film Noir." *Film Comment.* Spring, 1972: 8-13.

Thomas, Tony. *Music for the Movies.* Cranbury, NJ: Barnes, 1973.

Thompson, Kristin. *Breaking the Glass Armor: Neoformalist Film Analysis.* NJ: Princeton University Press, 1988.

Tierney, Gene and Mickey Herskowitz. *Self Portrait.* NY: Wyden, 1979.

Tuska, Jon. *Dark Cinema: American Film Noir in Perspective.* Westport, Conn.: Greenwood, 1984.

_____. *The Detective in Hollywood.* NY: Doubleday, 1978.

Warshow, Robert. *The Immediate Experience.* NY: Atheneum, 1970.

Whitney, John S. "A Filmography of Film Noir." *Journal of Popular Film.* 5 (1976): 321-371.

INDEX

A
Academy Awards iii, 37, 61
Algonquin Hotel 4, 8, 41, 53, 59
Anderson, Judith 38, 59–60
Andrews, Dana 57–58, 60–61, 66
antique French clock v, 2, 3, 5, 9, 47 35, 52
antique walking stick iv–v, viii, 24, 55
Archer, Eugene 84
Auberjonois, Rene 67
Aunt Sue 21–23, 31–32, 48, 62 (see Anne Treadwell)

B
Bambi 26, 30
Belton, John ix
Bennett, Joan 45
Bernstein, Elmer ii, 18
Bessie 4, 6, 9, 13–14, 22, 31, 35, 50–51, 62, 67, 87
Bettelheim, Bruno 83–84
Big Sleep, The viii, 28
Bouvier, Lee 64–65
Brahm, John 37, 64
Brubeck, Dave 40
Brute Force 81–82
Burnett, Carol xii, 68

C
Cain, James M.
Capote, Truman 64
Carpenter, Shelby v, 4, 8, 21, 31, 87
   the movie v, ix, 4–10, 12–16, 18, 23, 35, 37, 40–44, 46–51, 57, 59, 61, 75, 80, 86–87
   the novel 9, 18, 21–24, 29–33, 35, 44, 47, 86–87
   the play 10, 62–63
   the teleplay 64
Casablanca 19, 73
Caspary, Vera iii–iv, 24, 31, 39–40, 61–62
Chandler, Raymond 28, 33
cigarette case 7–8, 23, 50, 57
cinema noir 78–80
clock (see antique French clock)
Clooney, Rosemary 40
Collier's 21, 61
Conner, Chris 40
Conrad 22, 26–27
Corey, Lancaster 43, 51, 87
Coward, Noel 25
Crawford, Joan 61, 86
Cregar, Laird 37, 55

D
Dark Corner 65, 79
Dark Mirror, The 11
de Tocqueville, Alexis 85
decadence 60, 67, 79
decadent 12, 17–18, 26, 75
Designing Woman 87
Dietrich, Marlene 62
Dorgan, Danny 62–63
Double Indemnity 17, 45, 78
Dowson, Ernest 16–17
Dratler, Jay 37, 40–41, 46, 61
Dressed to Kill 87

Dunaway, Faye 67

E
Eliot 31
Ellington, Duke 38
Eyes of Laura Mars, The 67

F
Fallen Angel 34, 66–67
fat men 55
fat villain 35
film noir ii, 79
fin de siècle 33, 75
Final Script xii, 46–47, 50–51, 55, 90
First Draft xii, 37, 40, 45, 47, 49–52, 55, 90
Forties melodrama 45
Francis, Arlene 64
From Reverence to Rape 56

G
Garner, Errol 40
Gatsby 86
Gershwin, George 25
Gibbon 28, 35
globe, glass v, 24, 33, 35, 40–44, 47, 62
Going My Way iii, 61
Granger, Farley 64–65
Grappelli, Stephane 40
Gulliver's Travels

H
Hangover Square 45, 67
Haskell, Molly 56
Haymes, Dick 40, 49
Hays Office 76

Haywood, Eddie 40
Hoffenstein, Samuel 37, 46, 61
Hopkins, Miriam 63

I
I Wake Up Screaming 56
Ivanhoe 34

J
Jacoby vi, 5, 7–8, 32, 34, 42, 49, 57, 86
Jones, Jennifer 37
Jones, Tommy Lee 67
Johnson Office 76

K
Kenton, Stan 40
Kern, Jerome 25, 30, 55
Korman, Harvey 68
Kruger, Otto 63–64

L
Lady From Shanghai 11, 45, 79, 88
Lamarr, Hedy 37
Lardner, Ring Jr. 37, 46, 90
La Shelle, Joseph 38, 59, 61, 67
"Laura" xi, 84
Laura
  the character   ii–iv, vii–ix, xi, xii, 1–4, 6–11, 13, 17, 29–30, 33–35, 37–39, 44–46, 49–50, 55, 58–59, 75–77, 81, 84, 86–88
  the movie   ii–v, vii–xii, 1, 5, 13, 17–19,

the novel	22–23, 35, 37–53, 59–61, 65–67, 73–88
the novel	ii–iv, xi, 5–6, 19, 21–37, 43–44, 46, 77
the song	ii–iii, xi–xii, 1–2, 10–11, 18, 39–40
the play	ii, xii, 19, 59, 61–64
the teleplay	ii, xii, 19, 64–65

Lavagetto, Cookie 30, 47
Lawrence, Steve 68
Leave Her to Heaven 66
Leonard, Elmore 68
Lydecker, Waldo

the novel	iv–v, xi, 3, 6, 18, 21–28, 30–35, 39, 44, 46, 52, 55–57, 73, 77–78, 81
the movie	v–ix, xi, 2–10, 13–19, 23, 35, 37–44, 46–53, 85
the play	61–64
the teleplay	64

Lynch, David 88

M

Magnum P.I. xii, 67–68
Maltese Falcon, The vii, 19, 28
Mamoulian, Rouben 37–38
Martin, Freddy 40
McPherson, Mark

the movie	v–xi, 2–19, 23, 35, 37, 39–44, 47–53, 57–59, 74–77, 80–81, 83, 87
the novel	xi, 13, 21–29, 31–35, 44, 57–58, 78, 81
the play	62–64
the teleplay	64

McShane, Ian 67
Menuhin, Yehudi 40
Mercer, Johnny ii-iii, xii, 39
Montagnino's 8, 27–28, 39, 41–42, 49

N

necrophilia 13, 26
necrophiliac 50
noir iii, 17, 34, 45, 61, 78–80, 90

O

Oscar iii, xii, 61, 66–67, 86

P

Panofsky, Edwin 74
Parker, Charlie 40
Peterson, Oscar 40
Petrarch 1
Picture of Dorian Gray, The 2
Portrait

of Laura	iv, vi, 1–2, 6–8, 10, 31–32, 35, 39, 43, 62, 65, 74–75
as motif	x, xii, 1–2, 45, 59
Speicher & Sargent	32

Portrait of Jennie 2
Praz, Mario 26
Preminger, Otto iii, ix, 3, 34, 37–39, 52, 58, 61, 66–67, 91
Price, Vincent 59
Production Code vii, 76

Pygmalion 8, 41, 49

R
Raksin, David ii–iii, 11, 38–39, 66
Rashomon
Rebecca 1–2, 34, 59, 65
Redfern, Diane iv, 7–8, 10, 13, 22–23, 29–33, 43, 57, 62
Reed, Rex 65
Reinhardt, Betty 37, 46
Ring Twice for Laura 21, 89
Roberta 26
Robinson, Edward G. 45
Rugolo, Pete 40

S
Sablon, Jean 40
Sanders, George 64
Sargent, John Singer 25, 32
Sargentesque 1
Shakespeare 25
Sharkey's Machine iii, xii, 68, 88
silver cigarette case (*see* cigarette case)
Sklar, George 62, 64, 89
"Smoke Gets in Your Eyes" 41–42, 68
Someone to Watch Over Me iii, xii, 68, 87–88
Speicher, Eugene 25, 32
Stack, Robert 64
Stevens, K.T. 64
stick iv, 9, 33, 35, 43
Sutherland, Joan 40
Svengali
Svengaliesque 67
Swift, Jonathan 35, 55

T
The Great Gatsby 86
This Gun For Hire 56
Tierney, Gene 34–35, 37–38, 59–61, 66, 82
Tjader, Cal 40
Treadwell, Anne 4–7, 9–10, 12, 38, 40–41, 46–49, 51, 59, 62, 64, 87
Treadwell, Sue 21–23, 31–32, 48, 62, 64
Treadwell, Susan 23 (*see* Anne Treadwell)
Turner, Frederick Jackson 85
Twentieth Century Fox iii, 37
Twin Peaks 88

V
Vertigo iii, x, 1–2, 65, 87

W
Waldo (*see* Waldo Lydecker)
walking stick v, viii, 9, 24, 27, 39, 43–44, 52, 63
Webb, Clifton vi–vii, xii, 38, 60–61, 65–66
Welles, Orson 11
Weston, Paul 40
Where the Sidewalk Ends 66–67
Wilson iii, 61
Woman in the Window 2, 45, 83
Wooley, Monty 37
Woollcott, Alexander 21

Y
"You'll Never Know" 69

Z
Zanuck, Darryl iii, vi, 37–38,
 49, 52, 83

www.ingramcontent.com/pod-product-compliance
Lightning Source LLC
Chambersburg PA
CBHW030118010526
44116CB00005B/299